Also by Margot Leitman

Gawky:
Tales of an Extra Long
Awkward Phase

LONG
STORY
SHORT

WITHDRAWN

LONG STORY SHORT

THE ONLY STORYTELLING GUIDE YOU'LL EVER NEED

Margot Leitman

SASQUATCH BOOKS
SEATTLE

Printed in the United States of America

Published by Sasquatch Books
19 18 17 16 15   9 8 7 6 5 4 3 2 1

Editor: Hannah Elnan
Production editor: Emma Reh
Cover design: Mikko Kim
Lettering, illustration, and interior design: Joyce Hwang
Copyeditor: Elizabeth Johnson

Library of Congress Cataloging-in-Publication Data
is available.

ISBN: 978-1-63217-027-9

Sasquatch Books
1904 Third Avenue, Suite 710
Seattle, WA 98101
(206) 467-4300
www.sasquatchbooks.com
custserv@sasquatchbooks.com

SUSTAINABLE FORESTRY INITIATIVE

Certified Chain of Custody
Promoting Sustainable Forestry

www.sfiprogram.org
SFI-01268

SFI label applies to the text stock

For all of my brave students over the years.
You have inspired me daily.

CONTENTS

AUTHOR'S NOTE

This book should be read with a notebook, tablet, or laptop handy so you can play along and do the exercises. My wish is that this book inspires you to start jotting down some of your own stories. Or you can be a rebel and write all over my book. That's okay by me. I like rebels. They usually make good storytellers.

INTRODUCTION

To hell with facts! We need stories!
—KEN KESEY, author

In my early days as an aspiring actress in New York City, I was constantly running to auditions, hoping I wouldn't blow it due to my bad hair day/giant pimple/choosing to watch *Golden Girls* reruns instead of preparing my lines. I was constantly juggling two to three part-time survival jobs, usually some variation of terrible temp, unqualified substitute teacher, and "rude because I was exhausted" bartender. One day, while racing to get ready in time for a last-minute audition that I had to cancel a day of making twelve dollars an hour for, I burned my neck with a curling iron. It looked like I had a giant hickey. There was no makeup that could cover it up; I had to just go with it. Feeling really self-conscious when I walked in the room, I immediately said to the casting directors, "In case you're wondering, this isn't a hickey—it's a curling iron burn. I wish it were a hickey. I've had horrible luck with men lately." The casting director then asked what I meant, and I told a story of a dating disaster that had just occurred, and how after a bland vegan dinner out, my date and I split the bill and I had to watch him balance his checkbook at the table. Who does that?!

I made them laugh before I even read the script. A few days later, I got a call saying I got the part. I was thrilled to be working and didn't even realize that it was more likely that my personal story got me the role, not my acting chops. (Meanwhile, I remained single for another year.)

At that same time, I was also doing a lot of stand-up comedy. I was lucky enough to be booked on shows regularly, but the day of, I would have this overwhelming desire to cancel. I felt so much anxiety over doing stand-up; it was so obvious to both my mind and my body that it wasn't right for me. Then one night on a booked stand-up show that I somehow managed not to cancel on, I decided to throw my set away last-minute, and due to a little liquid courage (this show provided free drinks to comics), I riffed a true story from my disastrous love life on the spot. Unlike stand-up, there were no real jokes in my performance. I had no setups or punch lines. I just recalled the experience, which was a major calamity when it happened, but had become quite funny to me over time. And it killed. Sure the story was a little off-color and raunchy, but that wasn't why it worked. It worked because I was being both real and vulnerable.

~~~~~~~~~~~~~~~~~~~~~~~~~~~~

After my first foray into telling stories onstage, I managed to get booked on a storytelling show. I didn't even know there was such a thing. It was called *The Nights of Our Lives* at the Upright Citizens Brigade Theatre in New York City, and at the time I am writing this, it's still a regularly running show. I told a story I had told countless times socially, the story of the most embarrassing moment of my life, where I humiliated myself in front of the cheerleading captain of my high school. But when I told it onstage, the audience was silent for the first five minutes of my tale. I felt like I was bombing, until I realized that the audience was listening. When I finally got a laugh, five and a half minutes in, it was the biggest, longest laugh I had ever received onstage. It was one of those laughs that goes into applause, then back to laughter—a reaction I had never received in the six years I had been pursuing stand-up. It was such a rush; I couldn't wait to get booked on a storytelling show again. But the problem was, at that time, there were barely any storytelling shows. So, with the help of fellow comedian Giulia Rozzi, I cocreated my own. Because I was actively dealing with dating struggles (have I mentioned yet that my love life was a disaster?), we decided to theme the show around love/sex/dating and call it *Stripped Stories*.* We thought the word "stripped" was provocative, yes. But it also spoke to the sheer honesty behind telling a story onstage; you are stripping away the small talk and BS and getting to the nitty-gritty right away. Our very first show sold out; there was even a line half a block long of people who were turned away. People wanted to hear people tell stories. And they still do. Our show has been running for eight years now, and touring nationally, and we see no signs of it stopping.

I had a natural knack for storytelling. It just seemed like the perfect fit for me. I explained to my talent manager at the time that I was thinking of transitioning out of stand-up comedy. I told him I didn't really want to tell jokes; I wanted to tell true stories. He told me it was a

---

* Hey, it worked for Xtina!

dead end. My manager explained that a lot of stand-up comedians didn't want to be stand-up comedians, but it was what they had to do to get seen so they could become actors or television personalities and so on. I saw his point but tried to push forward, asking, "But couldn't telling stories lead to all that too?" He told me no one "just tells stories." I said, "What about David Sedaris? He sells books, and does live tours where he just reads his true stories, and he's a household name. I'd like to be the next David Sedaris." My manager said, "No. You're going to have to keep doing stand-up. Sorry."

Needless to say, I started seeing a therapist to "break up" with stand-up (we'd been dating for six years, and neither of us was happy—the relationship was going nowhere) and pursue a risky career path in something called "storytelling" that I wasn't even sure existed. Within a year of that awkward conversation with my manager, we had parted ways. By the following year, my next manager signed with me *because* I was a storyteller. Storytelling had become so popular it was something talent representatives desired, rather than tried to shut down. And I am still with that "new" manager, who is now my agent.

> Go where you are
> celebrated, not tolerated.
> **—UNKNOWN**

I am still a far cry from "the next David Sedaris," and that's okay. What matters is that I have been able to pursue the art form I truly love. It kind of makes me wonder how many others have been shot down when presenting what seems to be a cockamamie idea to their team: "What do you mean you want to put peanut butter and chocolate together and sell it as candy? One is sweet and one is savory—how can that possibly work?"*

I wanted to share this art form with others, so I started teaching classes. At first, I had to beg to get four people to take my class. But I stuck with it, and in under a year I moved my practice to the Upright Citizens Brigade Training Center, where I created two advanced levels in addition to a beginner level. My classes were suddenly

---

* Can you tell I am on a no-sugar diet as I am writing this book? There will be more discussion of the brilliance of Reese's Peanut Butter Cups later on in this book, I promise.

selling out within minutes of being posted. People wanted to tell their stories, and they wanted the tools to do so.

I no longer live in New York; I'm a California girl now, but my teaching practice has grown exponentially. I have literally been flown around the world to teach people how to tell stories. I could bore you with my entire résumé, but let's just say, when it comes to teaching people how to tell stories, I know what I'm talking about. I have taken some of the worst, most fearful public speakers ever and turned them into storytelling superstars. And I can do that with you.

I can honestly say that when I started storytelling—speaking openly about my experiences—my life changed for the better. I started having sincere relationships with people right away, instead of hiding behind bravado or small talk. I've drawn a lot of open, like-minded folks into my life since, and I've tried my best to cut the phonies out. I found ways to translate storytelling into work opportunities: books and screenplays, live shows, printed articles, teaching, public speaking, even corporate training. I also want to note that I did not have a financial cushion, like a trust fund or sugar daddy to fall back on while I pursued this.* I pursued storytelling while holding down multiple survival jobs (all of which I was terrible at), so I know it's totally possible

---

* I mean, who even has an actual sugar daddy?

for anyone to foray into this. After I started telling stories regularly, my finances changed. I was no longer a starving artist; I was constantly employed!*

Q: That sounds great, but you were an actress and comedian first. I'm not a performer. How does this apply to my life?

A: Stories play out in the business world too. For example, Steve Jobs utilized a lot of the principles of storytelling when speaking to consumers and the press.

In 2007, when unveiling the iPhone at Macworld, Jobs gave a brief intro about previous Apple products that helped shape the world. This served as the beginning of his story. Note that he did *not* launch into how he was forced to drop out of college for financial reasons or how he started the company—instead, he kept his intro to Apple's achievements.

A lot of first-time storytellers provide too much unnecessary information up top. When telling the story of a bad date, for instance, it's useful to give a synopsis of your dating history, but it has to be kept supershort, e.g., "I was

---

* Also, I am now married. That has nothing to do with storytelling, but I just wanted you to know the dating disasters finally ended, in case you were worried about me.

in a ten-year relationship throughout my twenties. When I hit thirty and was thrown back into the dating scene, I had no idea what I was doing." That's enough intro to get the audience to come on board.

In Steve Jobs's iPhone presentation, he made a joke about what he would be introducing, showing the audience a picture of an iPod with a rotary dial. His joke engaged the audience and brought them even more on his side. It also established a clear picture of what he was trying to do: reinvent the telephone.

When you're telling a story, if we don't know what you want—e.g., to meet your soul mate/make the team/start a family—we end up disinterested and not rooting for you. So be like Steve Jobs—tell us what you want! It can even be a silly or seemingly inconsequential desire, like "I just wanted to eat the corner piece of the cake with the fondant flower on it."*

In the middle of his story, Steve Jobs goes into great detail about his new product. He breaks it down into layman's terms so we can all understand what we need to know about how the iPhone works. But he knows his audience—he skips the technical jargon that only

---

* This is something I really want, and despite being at children's birthday parties about every other weekend, some hungry toddler always beats me to it.

VISUAL AIDS IN STORY-TELLING ARE LIKE NUDE SCENES IN FILMS: TOO MUCH IS OVERKILL programmers would get. His language and delivery enable him to connect with a worldwide crowd, and he uses visual aids only when necessary, never as a crutch.

Near the end of his presentation, Jobs's clicker malfunctions and his slide does not appear. And guess what he does? He tells a funny personal story from his high school days to kill the time. You can tell from his easy delivery that he had the story in his back pocket, that he had probably told it socially dozens of times. I encourage you to have a few of these ready to go, just like Jobs.

Steve Jobs concludes his speech by coming full circle, recounting Apple's inventions over the years and looking forward to the direction the company is going. He doesn't hit us over the head with a preachy ending, or insult our intelligence by telling us what we should have learned. He lets his presentation speak for itself, and you should too.

Jobs may not have revealed too much personally, but when he did, the audience reacted strongly. At one point he said, "I didn't sleep a wink last night. I was so excited about today." That's a feeling we can all relate to; it humanized Jobs and made him likable, which was part of his success.*

---

* That and the turtleneck. Who doesn't love a man in a turtleneck?

Here's the good news. All of these skills—from story structure to content, to what makes a story memorable, coherent, and engaging—can be learned.

Q: Umm, okay . . . so what is storytelling exactly? I tell stories with my friends all the time. Isn't that the same thing?

A: Live storytelling for an audience is a little different than social storytelling, but it uses a lot of the same skills. Whether it's for coworkers at a convention, a political speech, an audience at a comedy show, or in front of your congregation, good live storytelling has a formula. And while I can't teach you how to be funny (it's like rhythm—either you have it or you don't), I *can* teach you how to properly tell a story that will engage an audience and make them laugh at themselves through the eyes of the storyteller.

We see storytelling every day, even if we don't realize it. There are obvious examples, such as when someone has the office in stitches recounting an epically horrible date the night before. But we also see storytelling every night on talk shows, when a guest recounts a recent experience or when a host asks an author what inspired her novel.

And so . . . let's clarify exactly what storytelling *is*:

• **Storytelling is recounting a true experience from your life that has a beginning, a middle, and an end.** It could be about something big, like the moment you decided to quit drinking, or something much smaller, like the time your relative ruined your favorite Broadway show by talking too much throughout (I speak from experience). It doesn't matter how big or small your story is, as long as you were affected by it.

It also helps to define what storytelling *isn't*:

• **Storytelling is not a rant.** Talking to your audience for ten minutes about how the latest Martin Scorsese movie sucked is not a story. Telling us how you and your girlfriend broke up and to take your mind off the break up, you went to see the latest Martin Scorsese movie, and how every moment in that movie seemed to encompass exactly what was wrong with your relationship *is* a story. Your personal experience with the movie is the narrative.

• **Storytelling is not therapy,** though of course it can be therapeutic. This is a biggie. Remember, it's entertainment; no one should use storytelling as a substitute for professional help. "I just filed for divorce today from my douche-bag husband, and let me tell you what an asshole he was" is not a story. Five years later, telling the tale of the moment you realized you wanted a divorce *might be* a story. It all depends on your perspective and the structure of your tale.

• **Storytelling is not a substitute for a political platform.** If your audience expects to hear a first-person account and you instead go on about the importance of Occupy Wall Street, that's a political speech, not a story. Now, if the teller recounts a night camping out at Occupy Wall Street, and the experience has an underlying message, that's different.

• **Storytelling is not stand-up comedy.** You might get laughs in your story, sure, but you shouldn't force these laughs by sneaking in set-up/punch-line style jokes. If you do that, you'll risk sounding insincere. Let the story speak for itself, and if some laughs end up happening, think of those laughs as icing on the cake. Just save me the corner piece with the flower!

You'd be surprised how many recognizable and unexpected faces have dabbled in the live storytelling world. Darryl "DMC" McDaniels of Run DMC, author Malcolm Gladwell, political humorist Andy Borowitz, *Top Chef* judge Gail Simmons, sex advice columnist Dan Savage, and comedian Louis CK are just a few, and they all have amazing storytelling performances you can look up online.

So why should *you* read this book?

- Will you ever have to prepare a business pitch?

- Are you ever going to go on a job interview?

- Do you aspire to tell stories onstage?

- Will you ever have to make a speech at someone's wedding or funeral?

- Are you currently dating?

~~~~~~~~~~~~~~~~~~~~~~~~~~~~~~~~

I think that covers pretty much everyone. Have you ever been a guest at a wedding where the speech dragged on and made no sense to most of the people there? Don't be that person. I am going to give you all the tricks of the trade that will help you tell all the great stories you didn't even realize you had.

PART 1

~~~

GETTING STARTED

CHAPTER 1

YOU ALREADY HAVE GREAT STORIES

Most events in life can be
categorized in one of two ways:
a good time, or a good story.

—UNKNOWN

This is the quote I have hanging above my desk. I wish I knew who said it originally, but despite Googling it, I still have no idea. What I do know is it's the quote that defines the theme to my life.

Your mind is already filled with many "drop-the-mic"-worthy stories. You just have to unlock them.

Q: How do I unlock the incredible, emotional, and interesting stories within me? I'm not in a story-telling class, and I don't think there is anything interesting about me. I'm tired already and we're only on the first chapter. What's up with that?

A: Okay, here's the thing. You are numb to your own experiences. It's your life, you live it every day, and it's extremely boring to you. But it isn't boring at all. It's fascinating.

I once had a student say, "I don't know what's unique about me. I was in the army for ten years, and now I'm in LA with my husband, trying to be an actress, and that's about it." I was like . . . excuse me? Why did you join the army? How old were you? Did you realize you wanted to be an actress while you were somewhere in the trenches? Do flaky LA actresses annoy you because you have military discipline? Did you meet your husband in the army?

⋛ TELL YOUR STORY ⋚

Think about what people ask you about constantly. What aspect of your life are you asked about the most?

~~~~~~~~~~~~~~~~~~~~~~~~~~~~

For example, I have a son. So do lots of people. There is nothing unique about being a parent. But people ask me all the time how I balance my work and my child. The truth is, I don't. I have ridiculous meltdowns all the time, such as the day my four-month-old son went into hysterics while I was recording a live video chat for Deepak Chopra's YouTube channel, causing me to sign out of the *live* interview midway through. After my own hysterical cry about how I couldn't do it all, I managed to calm my son down, put on a fresh coat of hot-pink lipstick, and rejoin the interview five minutes later. The full version of that story, combined with the live footage (go ahead—look it up on YouTube), makes for a unique story about juggling career and motherhood. And when I told it onstage recently, I had to take multiple breaks for applause and laughter from the audience.

It wasn't being a mom that was interesting; it was my personal and vulnerable perspective on being a mom that was interesting.

REVEALING VULNERABLE MOMENTS FROM YOUR EVERYDAY LIFE ALMOST ALWAYS PAYS OFF

⋛ TELL YOUR STORY ⋛

Here's a quick thing you can do to see some of the stories already within you. Fill in this blank with true statements until you run out.

I AM _____.

~~~~~~~~~~~~~~~~~~~~~~~~~~~~

At first, your answers may be basic. For me, my initial responses might be:

I AM A BLONDE.
I AM LEFT-HANDED.
I AM TALL.

Boring, right?

However, the more I keep going with it, the more interesting my responses get.

I AM A FORMER HYPOCHONDRIAC.
I AM OBSESSED WITH GAME SHOWS.
I AM A SUPERFAN OF HAIR METAL.

Okay, now this is getting interesting. There's a great story that goes along with each of those facts about me. There's an anecdote that proves all those statements to be true.

~~~~~~~~~~~~~~~~~~~~~~~~~~~~

After you've exhausted all your I am statements, jot down a few notes next to the ones that have a corresponding anecdote. Then move on to part two:

I WAS _____ .

~~~~~~~~~~~~~~~~~~~~~~~~~~~~

The same thing will probably happen. You'll start with basic things. But usually, there is more than meets the eye in those first responses. One answer I get a lot in class is: "I was scared."

I always ask, "What scared you?" The answers often make a great story. Really think about *why* you answered the question the way you did. If you were scared of monsters, what is the whole story and what did it stem from? Personally, as a kid, I was scared of aliens attacking me when I took a shower. It stemmed from seeing the movie *Cocoon* at way too early an age because my parents thought that exposing me to all types of film, no matter how inappropriate, would make me more cultured—oh, wait a minute, this is becoming a story!

AN ANECDOTE is the SEED of a FULLY FLESHED-OUT STORY

WHEN IN DOUBT GO

DEEPER

You can always fill in your *I was* statements with weird jobs you once had. The answers are usually amusing: "I was a strawberry packer." "I was a plastic-hanger-maker supervisor." "I was an erotic dancer." The stories that go along with these answers are killer. So also be sure to answer *I was* with as many former jobs as you can think of, even if it was just a job for one day.

~~~~~~~~~~~~~~~~~~~~~~~~~

The final part of the exercise is this:

_____ IS THE STORY OF MY LIFE.

~~~~~~~~~~~~~~~~~~~~~~~~~

Don't get hung up on how huge this statement is. There's no right or wrong. Just answer it rapid-fire.

UPHILL BATTLE IS THE STORY OF MY LIFE.
PIMPLE ON THE BIG DAY IS THE STORY OF MY LIFE.
BLAZING MY OWN PATH IS THE STORY OF MY LIFE.

I once had a student answer this with "'Just a friend' is the story of my life." I stopped the group oral exercise to ask him more about this. He talked about how he gets in the "friend zone" with every girl he likes. I asked him

FIND THE RECURRING THEME IN YOUR LIFE, THEN LOOK FOR THE EXTREMES to tell the most extreme story he had about this. By the end of his impromptu example, I almost fell out of my chair laughing.

~~~~~~~~~~~~~~~~~~~~~~~~~~~~

Some of the most successful artists out there have found one recurring theme and told variations of that story over and over, to great success. Larry David has been the guy who says the one thing you're not supposed to say—via the characters George (based on himself) on *Seinfeld* and Larry on *Curb Your Enthusiasm*. Beyoncé sings about being a strong, independent woman in various ways. Sarah Vowell writes from the standpoint of a nerdy history buff in *The Wordy Shipmates*, *Unfamiliar Fishes*, and *Assassination Vacation*. Georgia O'Keeffe painted enough variations of blossoms to fill entire museum exhibitions.

⋛ TELL YOUR STORY ⋚

Write down a list of ten quirks about yourself.

~~~~~~~~~~~~~~~~~~~~~~~~~~~~

A sample list might start like this:

COMPETITIVE ONLY WHEN IT COMES TO DUMB STUFF

FABULOUS BAKER
LAZY ADVOCATE

Now, look at your list. Are there stories that explain these quirks? What was the dumbest competition you cared the most about? What makes you such a fabulous baker? What is the laziest thing you've done to help a cause compared to what you could have actually done to help? The stories should be pouring out of you at this point!

> *We all have a story about the craziest thing that ever happened to us, but the best stories often come from everyday life.*

Remember this the next time you question whether or not you are interesting enough to tell your tale!

"Boring damned people. All over the earth. Propagating more boring damned people. What a horror show. The earth swarmed with them."

—CHARLES BUKOWSKI, *Pulp*

DON'T HIDE YOUR QUIRKS – TAKE A CLOSE LOOK AT THEM. THEY MAY BE THE KEY TO A GREAT STORY.

A RECIPE FOR CREATING INTERESTING STORIES

Step 1: Don't be boring.*

Q: Have I become boring? Nothing interesting happens to me anymore!

A: Usually, your best stories are yet to be lived. But let's assess the situation here. When you were young, I bet you used to take more chances. You used to go out more, which created fuel for interesting stories. Perhaps you used to be single, which created funny dating and sex stories, and now you're married. Or you were a new parent, and now your children are grown. How will you tell another interesting story ever again? Maybe you used to live in New York City, where surprising things happened to you all the time, but now you live a more predictable life in the suburbs. Where will the new material come from once you've run out of stories from your crazy past?

Step 2: Live life for the story.

I am not a self-help guru by any means, so apologies if this gets a little self-help-y. But in order to be a great

---

* Also, you might not want to drink as much as Charles Bukowski. Just a suggestion.

storyteller, you must start saying yes to scary things again. Go to a party where you don't really know anyone. Go to your high school reunion. When a situation gets a little strange, as long as you aren't putting yourself in physical danger, try diving into the crazy instead of running from it. When you bump into someone from your past, perhaps someone who broke your heart, don't hide. Say yes to scary things! Say hi and see what happens. Don't get stuck in the rut of a monotonous life that nothing interesting ever happens in. In order to create more stories, you have to be open to new experiences.

Sure, I wound up with a great story one time just from going to get a manicure. I got into an argument with the manicurist, which ended with her saying, "You are horrible person. I *curse* you!" as I left the nail salon. And, yes, when one hour later my cursed manicure began peeling off—entire nails at a time—I knew I had a great story on my hands (fabulous pun intended).

But this scenario is actually the exception. I was passive in this situation, and 99 percent of my stories are about being active in a situation. Which brings me to:

Step 3: Don't wait for things to happen to you. Make them happen.

My favorite stories to tell are about active choices. Like when I said yes to marrying my now-husband after dating

WHEN THINGS START TO GET WEIRD, DIVE INTO THE CRAZY

only eight months. Or how I spent an entire summer at a
horseback-riding camp at age thirteen, despite having no
interest in horses.

As we grow older, we get comfortable in our lives, being
home on the couch, watching the same television shows,
taking the same route to work every day, staying at the
same job for years. Think about how many of your more
interesting stories take place somewhere other than your
house or apartment. How many take place somewhere
other than the town or city where you currently live?

People say to me all the time, "But crazy things just *happen* to you!" Maybe they do. But I believe a lot of it is that
I say yes when many others say no. Often when a conversation starts to get weird with a new person, our instinct
is to bolt. Maybe they're sharing too much. Maybe you'd
rather be scrolling through pictures of pie on Instagram.
Whatever the case may be, my theory is: as long as I feel
safe, I'll keep the conversation going.

So many great stories come from sharing intense
moments with strangers. Unlikely connections breed
beautiful stories. That's why we're all obsessed with those
pictures on the Internet of the hippo and the kitten that
are BFFs (or whatever unlikely animal friends you keep
stumbling upon in your news feed). So when someone is
trying to connect with you, let it happen. But preplan an

exit strategy in case it gets too weird for you to take. And if you sense danger, get out. No story is worth that!

I challenge students in every class I teach to stray from their routine, stand up to something that messes with them, do something out of their comfort zone, and so on. I get annoyed when people come in and say, "To stray from my routine, I watched a DVD instead of Netflix this week" or "I used my desktop instead of my laptop" or some other cop-out. Why not go for it! I had one student go as far as to get a tattoo (although I believe that guy was going to get that tattoo anyway and was just looking for the right excuse). But usually I find the best stories are when a person creates a challenge for himself/herself that is deeply personal. It was a challenge for one student to go to a bar alone and *not engage* with anyone, while another student challenged herself to go to a bar alone and *engage* with someone. Both got a good story out of it. So be brave! Do things that scare you. Don't cop out on life or you'll have no stories to tell.

> I have to live a life in order to tell a life.
>
> **—SPALDING GRAY,**
> **monologuist and actor**

NEVER PUT
YOURSELF IN
⚠ DANGER ⚠
FOR THE SAKE OF A
GOOD STORY

SIMPLE WAYS TO GENERATE MORE STORIES

1. Travel.

2. Switch the way you get to work every day—take a bus, carpool with a fun or quirky coworker, walk.

3. Say yes to more of the things that you are invited to.

4. If you are single, go on a date with an unlikely person.

5. If you are attached, convince your partner to do something adventurous with you.

6. Don't run from the weirdo at the party; engage with him/her.

7. Try a new method of exercising—make sure it's something you never thought you'd do.

~~~~~~~~~~~~~~~~~~~~~~~~~~~~

Q: Suggesting I try these story-generating ideas feels insincere, like I'm manufacturing moments just to have a story to tell. I don't want to cheat at storytelling, and isn't that cheating?

A: Do you think Elizabeth Gilbert would have written her best-selling book *Eat, Pray, Love* without making active choices and creating story-worthy moments in her life? That book never would have been written if she'd sat on her couch crying about the end of her marriage while eating Cheez Doodles and watching reruns of *Say Yes to the Dress*.

Did you know that the Beatles wrote between thirty to fifty songs during their visit to India to learn transcendental meditation? Do you think iconic songs like "Blackbird," "Mother Nature's Son," and "Revolution" would have been written from their La-Z-Boys? We don't judge the Beatles for doing something proactive to get inspired. There's no reason why you can't do the same! Besides, you never know what crazy memories (and great stories) will be triggered by an out-of-routine experience.

There is a difference between purposefully doing crazy things in order to manufacture a story and being open to new experiences that may or may not inspire a personal story from you. I have yet to hear a great story about a person going to work, coming home, and eating dinner in front of their DVR. Yet that's how so many of us spend our days.

I am a big fan of the television show *Project Runway*, in which fashion designers compete to create one-of-a-kind garments but are restricted by time/theme/materials/etc. pertaining to each episode's challenge. Cohost Tim Gunn often takes the designers to a museum, park, or landmark to get inspired. Many of the designers would never have come up with such brilliant ideas had they not taken time to soak in an unusual setting. Is that cheating? Or is it inspiration? I'm no fashion designer, but I imagine it's a lot harder to think of innovative clothing concepts from your couch.

> Look around you! Look out the window. Go for a walk. Go to a movie. Go to a museum. Go see a show. Read a book. Go to the library. Take the Circle Line. Have a conversation.
>
> **—TIM GUNN,** *Gunn's Golden Rules: Life's Little Lessons for Making It Work**

---

* From the "Get Inspired If It Kills You" chapter—worth taking a look at, as it applies to all forms of art.

CHAPTER 2
GETTING PAST FEAR

Our worst fears lie in anticipation.

**—DON DRAPER
(played by Jon Hamm),** *Mad Men*

Our worst misfortunes never happen,
and most miseries lie in anticipation.

—HONORÉ DE BALZAC, novelist

If I had to choose a favorite quote, this would be it. I like
both versions. Don Draper's more colloquial take works
for me when I'm trying to encourage a friend to take a
risk. Balzac's more eloquent version might hit home a

little more. But both apply tremendously to live storytelling. So many people never try live storytelling or public speaking because fear gets in their way.

Here are some of the fears I hear in every class I teach:

Q: I suck at writing. Don't I have to be a good writer to be a good storyteller?

A: It certainly won't hurt you as a storyteller to also be a good writer, but I don't believe it will give you a leg up either. Yes, in storytelling, you should eventually start writing your stories down in an informal manner that no one will ever see but you.* But before you even think about writing your stories down, there are lots of fun concepts to understand and explore. Focus on the process first; there is no need to worry about writing now. If the time comes, you'll have all the tools you'll need to make it less of a scary prospect.**

---

* For more on this, see Chapter 15.
** Writing a story for the stage is not a story that you intend to publish, so you can write it exactly how you speak, with slang and personal catchphrases only you would ever say. Writing for a magazine, website, newspaper, or book requires a different skill set than writing a story that is meant to be told. Lucky for you, writing for the stage is much easier!

Q: What if it gets back to the other person in my story?

A: Ahh. This is a big one. I hear this fear more than any other one, so listen up. You are in control of where your story lives. If you want it to live only on that stage, don't sign the release to allow it to be podcasted. Don't allow it to be videotaped and put on YouTube.

If you don't want your fourth-grade teacher to hear the story of how much you hated fourth grade, don't invite him/her to your show. And don't perform that story in a show located in your fourth-grade teacher's neighborhood.

Tell a story with a clean conscience.

Be smart about your characters. Change names, identifying characteristics, and gender. But your story should never just be about what an asshole your college boyfriend was. We've all behaved less than perfectly many times in our lives. You wouldn't want someone telling a story about what a jerk *you* once were, right? This would burn even more if you weren't there to defend yourself. Instead of telling the story of what an asshole your college boyfriend was, tell the story of what a fool *you* were for staying with him.

Remember, you are the star of your own story.

That's a pretty cool thought, right? In storytelling, it's all about you. Even if your entire story is about a past relationship—whether a work relationship, a creative collaboration, a romantic relationship, a family relationship—make sure your story focuses on you.

For example, I do have a story I tell about my college boyfriend. In the beginning of our relationship, my boyfriend, as he was falling asleep, rolled over in his bed and muttered "Good night, Diane." (For those of you who have forgotten, my name is Margot.) I then asked, "What did you just say?" To which he repeated, more coherently, "Good night, Diane."

Jerk, right? Well, not really. I'm the jerk for not leaving at that moment, for not walking back to my dorm room alone in the snow and knowing I deserved to be with someone who, at the very least, knew my name. I was the dummy for staying with this person for two more years and being shocked that he was cheating on me—I mean, he called me by the other woman's name in our first month together!

Now the story is about *my* journey, about who I was at the time (a wide-eyed college freshman) and my comically blatant (and willful) ignorance. I have also changed my ex's name, year in school, and major to protect his identity. I can recount my memory of a true story with a clear conscience.

In fact, I even have a funny story about this story. I prepared it for a live show once, and right before I went onstage I noticed that a college classmate of mine, someone who was very close friends with the "Good night, Diane" guy—a person who was the same year as him in school and the same major—was in the audience. I thought, "Oh no, this is awkward." But my story was completely true, except for the small changes, like name and major. So I went on with the story as planned, and afterward my former classmate came up to me to chat. He said, "I loved your story, especially because I know the references even more because I went to school with you. Now, are you going to tell me who that was about?" I was shocked. I said, "You mean you don't know?" To which my former classmate said, "I was a theater major. I didn't know anyone in the art department."

I couldn't believe it. By my changing that one small detail, I had completely disguised the other party's identity. Even his own friend didn't recognize him. My first thought was, "Wow, the 'Good night, Diane' guy and I dated a while in college—that's weird his friend forgot." Then I had a second thought, which was, "Oh, he doesn't remember because he has his *own* life and the last thing he's thinking about is who Margot Leitman was dating in 1999. I remember this story because it was a significant thing in *my* life, but no one else cares. They're all thinking about their own lives. Since college, this classmate of mine has been married and divorced, and I'm sure he's experienced tons of other significant personal experiences, which would lead him to not take up valuable brain space thinking about little old me."

I faced a lot of storytellers' biggest fear—getting caught—but because I was respectful of the other party in my story, no one got hurt. Also, I tell stories all the time, all over the world, and I can count on one hand how many times something like this has happened to me.

> *Storytelling isn't about bashing someone else; it's about being brave enough to share your story and make others feel better about their own lives.*

Let your audience leave feeling like "Wow, he/she went through that and he/she is standing up there laughing about it? I'm not doing so bad!"

I remember listening to David Sedaris's original recording of "SantaLand Diaries," where he hilariously, and famously, recounts his days working full-time as a Macy's holiday elf. At the time, I was thirty-two. I felt on top of the world after hearing his tale. I thought, "If David Sedaris—a

man who has published nine books, won the Thurber Prize
for American Humor, has performed to sold-out crowds,
and has had multiple *New York Times* best sellers—was an
elf at thirty-three, I am doing pretty damn great." Also, it
might help to point out that I was feeling pretty low that
day, having just spent a lot of time in Los Angeles and not
knowing how to get on my feet there. Sedaris succeeded at
one of the most important things a storyteller can do—he
made his audience (in this instance, me) feel better about
my own life via sharing his misfortunes.

> I have an appointment next
> Wednesday at noon. I am a
> thirty-three-year-old man
> applying for a job as an elf.
>
> **—DAVID SEDARIS,**
> **"SantaLand Diaries"**

The reality is your story will most likely not get back
to the other people in the tale. Especially when you are
first starting out. I always say to my classes, "I highly
doubt your mean college professor from the University of
Kansas is going to show up at your first show, which will
likely be at six thirty on a Monday in a theater under a

supermarket in New York." It's just not likely. It's also not likely that anyone in the yoga class you are teaching will be offended by your sharing a personal experience that relates to today's yoga set. The odds are pretty low that the story of your horrible boss, which inspired you to be your own boss and start your own business, will get back to him/her after you tell it at the small business owner's convention. These are paranoid thoughts. And to misquote the Kinks, "Paranoia will destroy you."

> For me, books have always been a way to feel less alone while being alone.
>
> **—JONATHAN AMES, author and creator of HBO's *Bored to Death****

Fun fact: David Sedaris has never been sued.

I don't think there is another living person whose true stories have been as widely read and heard as David Sedaris's. And no one has *ever* sued him.** So calm down!

---

* I believe the same could be said about watching or listening to a storytelling performance.

** I know this because an audience member at a live Sedaris show I attended asked him during the Q&A portion of the show if he'd even been sued and he said he had not.

Remember, "Our greatest fears lie in anticipation" ... or something like that.

I am living proof. I have a roster of about seventy-five stories. I have published a book of personal stories. At this point, I have told stories in front of tens of thousands of people over the years. My stories have played on the biggest storytelling podcasts, the ones with over one million subscribers, as well as on NPR. And interestingly enough, I have never told a story onstage and had the actual subject of the story be in the audience. So don't let the fear of a lawsuit get in the way of telling your story. It's not a very realistic prospect. Twice—and only twice, in my entire career—has anyone confronted me about telling a story involving him or her. After my story involving my childhood friend "Amanda" was broadcast on NPR and received tens of thousands of hits on YouTube (so quite a bit more widespread than a story told once onstage to a small crowd), "Amanda" e-mailed me. She wrote, "I just heard you tell a story on the radio, and I think I'm Amanda! I remember when that happened—it was so funny."

> Fear is . . . a kind of unintentional storytelling that we are all born knowing how to do.
>
> **—KAREN THOMPSON WALKER,**
> **novelist, from her TED talk**
> *What Fear Can Teach Us*

Because I told the story of *my* journey, not Amanda's, she really had no objections. Also, I was telling the truth.

The other story that got back to someone was a darkly funny tale involving an ex-boyfriend I'm on good terms with. Apparently he had been in a business meeting with someone when she somehow figured out that they both knew me in common. When the colleague figured out my ex was the subject of a story she once heard me tell, she repeated the story to him. When he contacted me later to tell me what happened, I asked, "Did it ruin your meeting?" "No," he said, "it did not." "Is this person going into business with you still?" He said that she was. I then asked, "Did you share a good laugh about it?" He said they did and he wasn't mad. In fact, it immediately bonded him with this colleague he is still in business with today. All because I kept my story true, and told it with a clear conscience.

See, my stories got back to the people involved and I survived. And no one got hurt!

> *Get rid of the "my mom will find my diary and read it" syndrome.*

In order to fully express yourself, pretend the boss/ex/friend/etc. your story is about is dead. It may sound harsh, but it's the only way to tell your story freely. You can always tone it down afterward. If you censor yourself before you begin, you'll never get anywhere.

Q: I'm too old to try something new. Maybe I should forget it. It's too late for me, right?

A: Wrong! Wrong! Wrong! Unlike ballet, sports, modeling, and acting, with storytelling, age can be an advantage.

The older you are, the more stories you will acquire, because more things have happened to you. You have more likely had your heart broken a few times, lived in more places, traveled more, and just experienced more life in general.

Even better, you will have the perspective (more on that in Chapter 8) to be able to talk about your past experiences with humor and ease.

One of my favorite students of all time started storytelling in his sixties. He once told a story of meeting Albert Einstein in an elevator. The entire class was blown away. A few months later, this student passed away suddenly on a train, on his way to a storytelling writers' group. As devastated as we were to lose him, we were so grateful that he had been brave enough to try something new and share his stories during his life. It would have been truly tragic if that story of meeting Albert Einstein had died with him. Now it lives on to all of us he told it to.*

Q: Why would anyone care about my life? I'm not famous or extraordinary in any way.

A: People will care about your life as long as it relates somehow to their own life. If you keep your story universal, the audience will be on board. Simply refuse to buy into the belief that you are not an interesting person.

〉   *Don't be afraid to be uncool.*   〈

---

* If you're on the younger side, don't worry—I've seen tons of young people succeed greatly at this form too.

I have seen crowds turn. It happens most often when storytellers are afraid to let down their guard and be real. Thinking you have to act cool may be a misconception that comes from the better-known world of stand-up. In storytelling, the jokes come naturally, from simply recalling the events that happened. A flippant, too-cool storyteller risks coming off as an unreliable narrator, who is just in it for the joke. So don't worry about laughs. They will come naturally. And if they don't come at all, that's okay too. Not all stories are funny.

> If you ain't desperate at some point in your life, you ain't interesting.
>
> **—JIM CARREY,**
> **actor and comedian**

Often at a stand-up comedy show, there is an antagonistic feel from the crowd, a "go ahead, try and make me laugh" arms-crossed stance. However, in storytelling, your audience wants you to succeed. They are not challenging you. Most likely, if you are telling a story onstage, you will be telling a tale to a nice group of NPR-listening, *New Yorker*-reading, Ira Glass–loving people. These people are there to hear you speak, and they cannot wait for you to shine. And the more real you are about your life experiences, the more they will love you.

> If you don't have your experiences in the moment, if you gloss over them with jokes or zoom past them, you end up with curiously dispassionate memories.
> —**DAVID RAKOFF**, *Fraud*

Think about talk-show guests. I recently watched a well-known movie star get interviewed on TV, and to every single question he was asked, he said something like, "Everything is great. My life is going great." He said nothing of substance, and what's more . . . I didn't believe him. By the end of the interview, I actually disliked him. This actor was afraid to be genuine, and the interview fell really flat. A few days later, I watched an interview with sitcom star Patricia Heaton. She spoke about her years of working a full day taping *Everybody Loves Raymond* and then coming home and working more, taking care of her four sons. She said her last son would go to bed and she would grab the wine and just "glug, glug, glug." In that moment, she was admitting that she struggled with having it all, that she was human, just like us—in fact, just like me, a working mother who has ended many a day with a big glass (or several big glasses) of wine.* By admitting she was less than perfect, she got me on her side.

⋛ TELL YOUR STORY ⋚

Try this fill-in-the-blank exercise to help launch you into fearless storytelling. Answer the questions with a response that's in what I call the "story zone"—not so safe that it will bore us, but not so personal that you would only tell a therapist. Don't overthink it, and do not make a list of answers. Instead, make a strong choice and stand by it. Don't get too caught up on the word "secretly." You don't have to write down a literal secret, but just something we might be surprised to know about you. Be honest.

THROUGHOUT MY LIFE, I HAVE BEEN
   HAUNTED BY _____.
EVERYWHERE I GO, I _____.
I SECRETLY LOVE _____.
I SECRETLY HATE _____.

---

* And that's with only one son!

Here are some sample answers I have gotten in the past that have inspired great stories:

THROUGHOUT MY LIFE, I HAVE BEEN HAUNTED BY THE BAD HAIRCUT I GOT IN COLLEGE.

EVERYWHERE I GO, I PLAN MY ESCAPE IN CASE OF A ZOMBIE APOCALYPSE.

I SECRETLY LOVE MY NEIGHBOR'S HUSBAND.

I SECRETLY HATE BEING A GIRL.

> *Fear is completely natural; it's ingrained in all of us. But so is storytelling. Even the cavemen did it!*

CHAPTER 3

THE TRUTH

Never let the facts get in the
way of a good story.

**—UNKNOWN (often attributed to
Mark Twain or Ernest Hemingway)**

I disagree! Even if Mark Twain or Ernest Hemingway did
say this, they were fiction writers. They weren't telling
true stories from their life. I would rephrase this saying to:
"Your story is only as strong as its truths."

I used to bartend for extra cash at the Upright Citizens
Brigade Theatre in New York City. The bar at the time
sold T-shirts, lighters, and other merchandise, including books. The book *Truth in Comedy: The Manual for*

Improvisation, by Charna Halpern, Del Close, and Kim "Howard" Johnson, was prominently displayed, as it was recommended for all improv students. Almost every night I worked, a customer would ask me if it was a good book. And I would always respond, "The book is great, yes, but the concept is right there in the title. Just think about it."

Okay, so maybe I'm a better writer/performer than I am a salesperson. But I stand by what I said. All you need to remember is right there in the title of the book. *Truth in Comedy*. Comedy comes from truth. And there is so much true material from your life just waiting to be told. So don't waste time worrying about fiction!

Q: Does my story have to be true? I think adding some made-up stuff would make it more interesting.

A: Don't make up your story. You know when a person is lying to you. Their eyes get shifty, and they speak at a higher volume or a faster pace. My husband always says, "I was getting a *Talented Mr. Ripley* vibe off of him" whenever someone seems to be pulling one over on him.* So don't you think your audience—whether a potential boyfriend/girlfriend on your first date, your colleagues

---

* *The Talented Mr. Ripley* is a great 1999 thriller, based on a classic novel by Patricia Highsmith, in which Matt Damon plays a charming sociopath named Tom Ripley.

at the company meeting, or the guests at your sister's wedding—is smart enough to see through a story that's supposedly true but really isn't?

Unless you are attempting a more folklorish style of storytelling, a form I know nothing about (and, by the way, you've purchased the wrong book if that's what you want to learn about), just stick with the truth. I get the "truth question" in every class I teach. I still don't completely understand why a person might think a lie would be more interesting than their real life, but I believe this is also based in fear. Just as fear can inhibit us from getting started, it can get in the way of being truthful. You may have a fear that your life isn't interesting enough, a fear that if you tell the truth you will be judged, a fear that you won't be considered cool if everyone knows who you really are.*

> I have a theory that the truth is never told across a desk. Or during the nine-to-five hours.
>
> **—HUNTER S. THOMPSON, journalist and author**

---

* As I said in Chapter 2, I assure you the opposite is true.

Think about it. Have you ever watched, read, or listened to someone who seemed like they were being dishonest with you? Perhaps you've seen a politician being less than candid about his past, or heard a story your friend boasts about at a party that seems too perfect to be true. People lie because they think it will be funnier or more interesting.

⋛ TELL YOUR STORY ⋛

Think of a few people who got caught lying about their lives. What was the public's reaction? Now think of five people who were honest. What was the public's reaction to that?

~~~~~~~~~~~~~~~~~~~~~~~~~~

I'll start you off. When Bill Clinton was asked about marijuana use in his past and he said, "I didn't inhale," no one believed him. In fact, one could argue, it made him less likable. When Barack Obama was asked about drug use in his past, he said, "When I was a kid, I inhaled . . . that was the point." The public basically went, "Umm . . . okay," forgot all about it, and went on with their lives. In storytelling, you will be celebrated for revealing the truth.

} *Trust the intelligence*
of your audience. {

In one of the first classes I taught, I had a student who was a pharmacist by trade. He told a story of a customer who had just gotten in a bad car accident coming in for a prescription. A few minutes later, a second customer came in, who happened to be the very person who'd hit the original customer's car, and they started screaming at each other in front of the pharmacist. I asked the story-teller (the pharmacist), "So then what happened?" And he said, "I took them both outside and they began physically fighting, so I decked them both." At this point, he lost his audience (the whole class). There was no way my student (the pharmacist) who was on duty would leave his post and get into a dual fistfight.

I believe that what actually happened was the two customers got in an argument and he asked them to take it outside, where they continued to fight. Perhaps he tried to break it up. Perhaps they simply had an argument at the counter. What this student didn't realize is that it was interesting enough to have two customers who had just gotten into a car accident show up at the same pharmacy. Often we think the truth isn't interesting enough. I assure you it is.

Q: But what if I don't remember exactly what happened? It's not like I recorded it. How am I supposed to truthfully recount dialogue that I don't remember?

A: No one expects you to remember every instance of your life perfectly. Besides, that would make any sane person go crazy. I am sure, however, that there are many moments or words that you will never forget.

If your story were for a printed entity, such as the *New Yorker* or the *New York Times*, you would be fact-checked, and you'd be shocked at the things they fact-check. If you were to write a story about your current marriage, and you mention in the printed story that your first kiss was with Becky Lawrence during a game of seven minutes in heaven, you better bet that the *New Yorker* will track down Becky Lawrence to verify whether or not she ever kissed you, and whether it occurred during said game. Stories told live are a whole other entity.

> *In live storytelling, there is no*
> *fact-checking. We just have to*
> *take your word for it.* *

So, in order to recount the story to the best of your ability, keep whatever true details in there that you can remember. For dialogue you can't remember, add in what you think someone *might* have said—meaning if you are telling the story of asking the girl of your dreams to the prom, and you remember a lot of back and forth with her before actually getting her to say yes, you might want to phrase it like this: "I finally got up the courage to ask her, and at first she said no. A week later, she changed her mind to maybe, and a week after that she said she'd go with me as long as I 'didn't make a big deal about it.'"

Don't get caught up in the minutiae. If you're telling the story of the time you ate a lot of pancakes and you can't remember exactly how many it was, it's okay to say you ate "seven" pancakes. No one is going to stand up and interrupt your whole story and yell, "Liar! It was five!" However, if you're telling the story of how scared you are of roller coasters, and you tell us that you finally overcame

---

* Unless you are lucky enough to get on Ira Glass's podcast/public radio show *This American Life* or something else of that caliber— in that case they will fact-check the heck out of your story.

that and went on the scariest roller coaster ever, when the truth is really you held your friends' purses while they rode the coaster and you thought about how much fun *they* were having, that's not okay. It's not okay to fabricate the plot of your story; it is okay to make the unimportant details more specific.

Q: What if the timeline of my story is confusing? Is it okay to fudge that to make the audience understand it all a little better?

A: I say yes! For example, I often tell a story that takes place at sleepaway camp. I went there for two glorious summers of my life. But that fact muddles the story I often tell about camp. It would be confusing and time-consuming in the middle of my story for me to stop and say, "And then camp ended for the summer, and I went back home, and then I enrolled again the following summer—this time for four weeks instead of three. So my second year of camp started, and all the same people were there, and . . ."

Could it get more boring than that? What I do instead is condense the timeline. For the sake of clarity, I frame it all as one seven-week summer at sleepaway camp. All the events take place in one summer, rather than two summers consisting of a three- and a four-week session. What matters is that the event, plot, and characters in my story are all accurate.

Q: What about extraneous characters? Is there a way to make the "cast list" of your story simpler without fudging the truth?

A: It's often a good idea to narrow down the number of characters in your story. Remember, you are the star. It's all about you! I don't care about your three housemates and their detailed backstory. Time after time, I've seen people spend three minutes describing every single person who worked in their office and they still haven't started the meat of their story. If your story is about you versus the horrible assistant your shared an office with, and there was actually an additional person who sat in your office who kept his head down, never spoke, and has nothing to do with your story, it's okay to never mention that another person was there. I always tell my students, if there were five people in the car, but the story is about the screaming fight you got in with your best friend—cut the other three people. What we care about is the fight you got in with your best friend, not wasted character descriptions that never pay off.

Also, there is something called a "composite character." A composite character is a conglomeration of different people who all represent the same thing squished into one fictional person. In my first book, *Gawky: Tales of an Extra Long Awkward Phase*, which was full of true stories from my teen and preteen years, two bullies were present throughout: Chad Decker and Jessica Rosenstein. Although my first book was a memoir, neither Chad nor Jessica were real people. "Chad" was a hodgepodge of all the male bullies I'd encountered in my teen years, and "Jessica" was all the female ones. What a special teenage experience I must have had to have been bullied by *so many* people! It would have been hard for the reader to keep track of everyone, so I created Chad and Jessica. That way, readers weren't confused by extraneous characters, and instead got to know two bullies in-depth.

> **TIP:** If there are too many people in your story who all represent the same thing, combine them into one.

Q: What if I don't remember exactly what movie I watched on the date, or what song was playing at the concert when we kissed? Can I make it up?

A: Sort of. Think of a movie that you *might* have been watching at the time, or a song you *could* have been listening to that fits the era. This may take a little Google research. You don't want to say you were at the drive-in watching *The Big Lebowski* if your story takes place in 1979.

Most audiences will agree it's more fun to hear about you making out on the couch while *Titanic* played in the background than you simply making out on the couch. In my memoir, *Gawky*, I recall having an impromptu dance party in a candy shop during the weekend of my prom. I didn't remember exactly what song was blasting, so I Googled hit dance songs popular in that era and decided on "C'mon N' Ride It (The Train)" by the Quad City DJ's, which created a vivid image of how fun the party was. I'll never be able to prove that was the song playing, but what matters is that the meat of my story is true. Now, if I had made up the whole story and I'd never danced in a candy shop, that would totally not be okay.

Q: Are there any legitimate ways to keep your story truthful while maintaining the privacy of the others in your piece?

A: There's nothing wrong with saying you met the friend in the story in college even though you really met her in high school. If that protects her identity, and the rest of your story is true, go for it. If your story is about an awful former boss, feel free to change his/her gender in the story to prevent it from getting back to him/her.

For example, I often publicly tell the story of the time one of my close friends tried to set me up with a very well-known contemporary sitcom star and how it went terribly awry. He's not a jerk in the story; it's just comical what a horrendous match we were. But this is tricky, as he's a public figure. So what do I do? I tell the story and say, "I can't tell you his name, but for the sake of the story let's just refer to him as 'Kirk Cameron.'" Not only does it get a laugh, it takes away the distraction of many audience members thinking, "I wonder who it is." Also, because I mentioned this was a contemporary sitcom star, not an '80s sitcom star, the audience is sure it is *not* Kirk Cameron ... Or was it?*

A great example of this identity-protection technique is Elna Baker's story about kissing married "Warren Beatty"** in her book, *The New York Regional Mormon Singles Halloween Dance*.

Another idea is, instead of calling the three people in your story Lenny, Karl, and Pete (which is a lot for an

---

* Just kidding—it really wasn't.
** Not really Warren Beatty.

audience to keep track of), try nicknaming them via interesting characteristics. It's a lot easier for an audience to keep track of Dreadlocks, Afro, and Hemp Necklace rather than Lenny, Karl, and Pete. Also, it gives us a fun visual and protects their identities. You can also nickname characters by using celebrity/public-figure look-alikes. Rather than saying, "Sally had a pudgy figure, round eyeglasses, and a bald spot," you could refer to the Sally character as a "female Ben Franklin." Name protected, laugh built in, and strong visual accomplished!

Try coming up with fun nicknames for the people in your stories.

> If you tell the truth you don't
> have to remember anything.
> **—MARK TWAIN***

≳ TELL YOUR STORY ≲

Write a list of the white lies you have told in your life. Don't worry—you don't have to show it to anyone.

---

* Now here's a quote that's definitely from Mark Twain, and it's one I can really get behind!

Here's mine:

• I PLAY GUITAR.

Nope. I suck at guitar. I want to play guitar. I love rock music. I took guitar lessons in high school and was never so shocked at my sheer lack of natural talent. I know a few basic chords and can fake it for about thirty seconds. But I am a far cry from Eddie Van Halen.

• I HORSEBACK RIDE.

Nope. I am actually terrified of riding horses. I went to a horseback-riding camp the summer between seventh and eighth grade, and on the first day of camp I managed to fall off a horse that was *standing still*. But I have auditioned for many commercials where they asked for "experienced riders."*

• I SPEAK FRENCH.

Okay, I took two years of French at the beginning of high school and had to drop out because I was failing. Then I dated a French guy for a bit who spoke fluent English, but I usually leave the "spoke fluent English" part out.

---

* None of which I booked.

It's so much sexier to imagine me speaking fluent French to my French lover.

• MY MOM IS BRITISH.

Well, my mom's mom immigrated here from England, so technically my mom is British, right? That's much more interesting than her being born in Pittsburgh.

Do you like me less now, knowing that I am not really a French-speaking, horseback-riding, British guitar player? I didn't think so.

I mean, who would want to be friends with that perfect, stuck-up-sounding person? I like people who are honest about themselves and their shortcomings, and I think you do too. So do audiences.

> Every time you come up with a strong satiric idea, the world tops it.
>
> **—DEL CLOSE,**
> **actor, teacher, and pioneer in**
> **long-form improvisation**

CHEAT SHEET FOR

CHANGING CHARACTER NAMES
& IDENTIFYING CHARACTERISTICS
(FOR PRIVACY)

RECONSTRUCTING
CONVERSATION SPECIFICS
("HE SAID")

GUESSTIMATING EXACT
NUMBERS, AGES, YEARS

COMBINING CHARACTERS

CONDENSING TIME

FUDGING THE TRUTH

MODIFYING THE PLOT

MAKING UP CHARACTERS

ALTERING THE STORY'S
EMOTIONAL TRUTH!

CHAPTER 4
THE UNIVERSAL THEME

As for unhappy families,
star-crossed lovers, and exiled heroes,
they are simply universal.

—ELIF BATUMAN,
The Possessed: Adventures with Russian Books
and the People Who Read Them

I am sure we all have this friend—the friend who talks
and talks and talks about his/her own life incessantly and
never asks about yours. You listen to him/her go on and
on and think, "When are they going to ask about me?" You
probably detest listening to this person. So in storytelling,
you must do everything in your power to prevent yourself

from being this person. Remember, *no one cares about your life.*

Q: But Margot, doesn't that counter everything you've already said? I thought people cared about my life and that's why I should share my stories?

A: You have to trick people into caring about your life. You have to somehow make them think that your life is just like theirs. Once you do that, they will listen to anything you have to say. You can't make your listeners feel like they're excluded from your story. They must feel like they're a part of it.

One way to do this immediately is to identify setting. So often I hear lengthy stories about a person's childhood and by the end of it I don't know if they grew up in rural Texas or urban Baltimore. By showing your audience where your story takes place, you immediately invite them into your world, whether they have a shared experience there or it's a place they've always wondered about. However, if you don't identify any setting, you will likely alienate a lot of your audience by making them feel left out.

Just recently I heard an engaging and supercreepy story from student Brian Neufang, which all took place on a farm in Washington State. Brian described the setting so well—the isolation, the primitiveness, the constant rain—that even though I have never even been to a farm in Washington (a far cry from the strip malls of New Jersey that I grew up near), I was transported right there. It was a place I had seen in movies and television, and I could relate in that way. Additionally, when Brian got to the creepy part of the story (it was a tale involving a Ouija board—enough said!), it was a lot spookier knowing he was on an old-fashioned farm in the middle of nowhere. It was like a scene right out of a horror movie, a genre I'm a big fan of, and so I really could relate to his piece in a way I probably wouldn't have without his clear definition of setting.

Q: How am I supposed to make strangers feel like they're a part of a true story that happened to me?

A: You can easily adjust the first few sentences of your story to make it universally appealing. First, you have to avoid statements that are noninclusive. Here's an example of a way I *could* start a story I tell often:

> "The craziest things always happen to me. One time, when I was studying theater abroad in London, my friend Natasha and I had the wildest night ever . . ."

In these two sentences, I have alienated most of my audience. Here's how I managed to do that:

"The craziest things always happen to me."

Wow, her life must be so exciting. Nothing crazy ever happens to me. I'm just an average person with a normal life. She's nothing like me; I'm going to tune out.

Chances are, if you respond well to something, it's because you relate to the person. If you don't respond well, it's because you feel like you aren't included. For example, I lived in New York City for eleven years, but despite the show *Gossip Girl* taking place there, I have never seen a single episode. That show was about wealthy, elite teens on the Upper East Side. I never lived on the Upper East Side, I didn't live in New York City as a teenager, and I certainly was never wealthy when I lived there. My New York City life was a broke twentysomething's journey downtown. I just wasn't interested in *Gossip Girl*. Since it didn't include me, I never gave it a chance.

On the flip side, despite having no interest in football and not being from Texas, I have seen every episode ever of *Friday Night Lights*. That show, which takes place in a middle-/working-class football-centric small town, *did* relate to my upbringing, even though my small town was in New Jersey and, to be honest, I hated how much everyone cared about football. I like that show because I relate to a town being really prideful of its high school team, and the struggles middle-class America faces.

Let's go back to my story and see how I alienated my audience with my second line:

> "One time, when I was studying theater abroad in London, my friend Natasha and I had the wildest night ever . . ."

Wow, she's a total theater snob who was rich enough to study abroad in the expensive city of London. I bet she and her rich friend Natasha had a crazy and expensive night that I could never have.

Now, while keeping my story true, look how easy it is to flip the first few lines of my story into something that relates more to the general population. I can tell the same story, but instead begin like this:

> "Have you ever run completely out of money? Your bank account hits zero, and that zero is actually a zero. There is no emergency credit card, no call you can make to a parent—you're just at zero. I hit zero when I was studying abroad in London, and conveniently, my visiting friend Natasha also hit zero that very same night. We decided to take our subway passes and go hit the town anyway."

By starting with a question (which is a fun way to start a story but not a rule to abide by), I invite the audience into my world. When someone does that conversationally— as in "My boss wants to be friends outside of work, but I want to keep it professional. Has that ever happened to you?"—you feel like the person is conversing *with* you rather than talking *at* you. Also, by admitting I was a broke student studying abroad, rather than a posh princess, I am more relatable, and therefore, I am well on my way to engaging the audience with my personal story with universal themes.

⋛ TELL YOUR STORY ⋚

I call this "The Story Told a Thousand Times." Think of the story you have told the most often in your life. Everyone has one—your friends/family beg you to tell it so much you're sick of it. Got it? Now try to identify what exactly is universal about that story. Is it a universal feeling? Struggle? Common misconception?

~~~~~~~~~~~~~~~~~~~~~~~~~~~

I do this exercise with every single class I teach, whether it's a one-day workshop for hotel executives with no storytelling experience, or an eight-week class at the

Upright Citizens Brigade Theatre. What's universal about my wild-night-in-London story is: sometimes the best nights of our lives are not about fancy dining and evening gowns but good friends and a good spirit.

Remember, the stories you find yourself telling repeatedly in social situations are the one you should be exploring to develop more.

~~~~~~~~~~~~~~~~~~~~~

Believe it or not, the movie *The Shawshank Redemption* is a nearly perfect example of storytelling. Don't believe me? I'll show you what they did and how it works.

Plot: Two imprisoned men find friendship in prison and eventual redemption outside prison walls.

Everyone can agree that's what happens in the movie. That's the plot of the story. Remember doing those pesky book reports as a kid? We've been identifying plot for a long time.

Now, let's move on to the universal theme, or message, of the film, which may be different for each person watching it. Here's my interpretation.

Universal Theme: Never give up.

Yours might be: Stay true to your convictions.

Or: True friends can be found everywhere.

Or: Eventually, if you are patient, redemption will come.

> It's my life.
> Don't you understand?
> IT'S MY LIFE!
>
> **—ANDY (played by Tim Robbins),**
> *The Shawshank Redemption*

The Shawshank Redemption's success is due to its appeal to all of us. Yes, it's the story of Andy's life, but it's also our story. Hopefully, not many of us have been wrongfully imprisoned for most of our lives, but what appeals to us about the movie is the relatable themes: frustration, anger, injustice, loyalty, and hope.

There's one more thing we can break down in a story/movie. I call it the "point of entry." That's the point where your story somehow pertains specifically to someone else's life. This is different for every person in the audience. The point of entry is where our attention is really piqued; it's what should keep us engaged throughout.

Point of Entry: For me it is when the character of Red (Morgan Freeman) is introduced. Although I have, luckily, never been imprisoned, I, too, have felt like an outsider in a new place, as Andy (Tim Robbins) did. The friendship between Red and Andy reminds me of how I felt when I first moved to the intimidating city of New York and began waiting tables for the first time. Everyone who worked at my restaurant was jaded, with years of experience in the restaurant industry, not to mention stunningly model-worthy beautiful. I kept messing up and was getting eaten alive. I thought I was going to be fired. Then, on my third day, a hilarious, stand-up comedian named Danny came in to work his shift. He made me laugh; he helped me learn the ropes and calmed me down, and was my first friend in postcollege real life. We are still friends to this day.

For someone who has experienced infidelity, the point of entry in *The Shawshank Redemption* may be the moment Andy's wife cheats on him. For someone who has been imprisoned, the point of entry may be when Andy first walks into the prison. Since everyone's point of entry is different, a good story has many points of entry.

So let's recap.

- **Plot:** What happens in your story. Think of this like a *TV Guide* description of your story. (Should be the same for every listener.)
- **Universal Theme:** The message behind your story. (May vary by listener.)

• **Point of Entry:** The moment the listener applies your story to his/her *own* life and becomes even more engaged. (Will vary by listener.)

> *We are all selfish. Unless your story is also our story, we won't give it a chance.*

Here are some examples of extreme stories that were very successful because there was something universal about them.

• ***Breaking Bad:*** Are you a meth dealer? I hope not. So why was this such a widely viewed show? Universal themes include: An underachiever finally overachieving at something. Unlikely friendships. Blurred lines regarding whom the bad guy really is.

• ***The Wizard of Oz:*** My guess is you've never been thrown into the air into a magical munchkin land by a tornado. So why is this a classic? Universal themes include: There's no place like home. Everything you need, you already have; you just need to believe in yourself. Sometimes the people in charge have no idea what they're doing.

• **Homer's *Odyssey*:** Oh, you didn't fight in the Trojan War? Your family never assumed you were dead after the

UNLESS YOUR TALE CONTAINS A UNIVERSAL THEME, IT'S BEST LEFT WITH YOUR THERAPIST OR YOUR BEST FRIEND

TRICK US into LISTENING by MAKING US THINK IT'S all ABOUT US

fall of Troy? So why is this poem, composed in the eighth
century BC, still widely read today? Perhaps because of its
themes of homecoming, identity, and temptation. Haven't
we all struggled with at least one of those issues?

> **TIP:** The next time you're watching a
> scripted TV show or movie, or reading a
> book, and you're really enjoying it, think
> about *why* you like it. How does it apply
> to your own life? What are the universal
> themes? Be sure to do the reverse too. If
> you don't like something, why not? I bet
> it's because you don't feel included.

CHAPTER 5

THE THESIS-BASED STORY

The best way to do something is to do it.

**—A quote on a card I gave
an ex-boyfriend who never got out of
bed to make it to class on time***

Q: How do I start my story?

A: Beginnings are hard. This is why so many of us stay in jobs we don't like, relationships that aren't working, etc. We do this because the prospect of beginning something new is often scarier than sticking with

---

* He flunked out of school soon after. I guess my card didn't work.

something old and stale. My literary agent has a tattoo that says "Begin anywhere." Of course someone in the book business would have this. In that world, often the hardest part is simply starting to write.

So where does one begin a story? First, let's think about how *not* to start a story. Now, this is just my personal preference, but I hear a hell of a lot of stories started in a certain overdramatic, rigid, impersonal way. I see it all the time, and it goes a little something like this:

> "January 2013. Now a thirty-year-old man, a father myself, I stand before my childhood bedroom, looking for remnants of days past. I glance around the room and see him—Snowy, my white teddy bear— and it all comes back.
>
> "As a kid, all I ever wanted was a teddy bear. My brother, ten years my senior, was way beyond the teddy-bear phase."

I just don't get this technique. Why are we starting with this impersonal opening, which is not the way anyone speaks? Why not just start your stories like you're conversing with a group of friends? Why does telling a story have to be so formal? It's not a dissertation. Going back to the iPhone launch, Steve Jobs certainly didn't start with an unnatural overwritten beginning. He began talking about the iPhone by taking a deep breath and saying, "This is a day I've been looking forward to for two and a half years." I think we can all relate to that. Whether it's our wedding day, or the day our baby is born, or the day we finally get promoted. We all understand what it's like to wait and wait for an exciting moment to happen. That's such a better way to lure us in than to say:

> "February 2005. The snow falls in Toronto as I stare at the tiny screen of my flip phone, thinking, 'Why isn't this enough?'"

Option 1: Start your story with a little intro about yourself and then get right into it.

Here's what I mean, going back to the teddy-bear example:

> "As the youngest kid in a big family, I was always trying to fit in and be cool way beyond my years. My oldest brother was on the football team, and he teased me relentlessly if I ever did anything too babyish. What he didn't know was I sucked my thumb until I was eight, snuck in episodes of Sesame Street when no one was looking, and had a secret best friend . . . Snowy the magical teddy bear."

Do you see how much easier that is to picture, rather than the stoic, impersonal original intro?

Option 2: Start your story as if your audience is your best friend and you're letting your BFF in on a little secret.

This is one of my favorite ways to begin a tale. Instead of making a big to-do, I just take a deep breath and start talking as if we've all known each other for years.

For example, when telling the story of getting cursed by a manicurist*, I begin like this:

> "So, I'm not one to perpetuate stereo-
> types, but I'm from New Jersey, and I
> genuinely believe that a full set of acrylic
> fake nails, with airbrushed nail art and an
> optional nail piercing, is the true standard
> of beauty."

Also, note that I start the story with the word "so." I do this about 99 percent of the time. Starting a story with the word "so" makes me feel like I'm starting in the middle of a thought, like I'm midway through a casual conversation and I'm easing into the meat of a story I want to tell my friend. Feel free to try this yourself. A lot of my

---

* I mentioned this strange tale in Chapter 1.

students have told me that adding those two little letters, *S* and *O*, before launching into the nitty-gritty of it all, calms them down and makes it all feel a lot more conversational.

Option 3: Start your story with a thesis statement about yourself and then tell a specific story that proves your thesis to be true.

Remember writing term papers in college and declaring a thesis at the top and then writing a paper that proves it? As a theater major, I wrote fabulously pretentious papers like:

- "Freudian Themes in Sondheim's *Into The Woods*"
- "Iago's Repressed Homosexuality in *Othello*"
- "Modern-Day Themes in Aristophanes's *Lysistrata*"

The same technique works for storytelling, except . . . the thesis statement should be all about you. Make a declarative statement about yourself and then tell a specific story that proves it.

But that's easier said than done. The thought of finding a thesis statement for your life can be quite overwhelming.

⋛ TELL YOUR STORY ⋛

So let's narrow it down.

Make a thesis statement about your love/sex/dating life, then tell a story that proves it.

If that's too tough to narrow down, declare a thesis statement about your relationship to travel or money.

Between love/sex/dating/travel/money, you must have something.

~~~~~~~~~~~~~~~~~~~~~~~~~

Here are some examples:

- I am afraid of commitment.
- I am a serial monogamist.
- I'll stay in a relationship I'm miserable in just to avoid the confrontation of breaking up.
- I become a different person when I travel.
- When it comes to money, I either have too much or too little.
- Just when I think I'll never make any money ever again, something unexpected comes through.

Feel free to go beyond these categories; I just find it helps to narrow it down.

Once you have figured out a declarative statement about yourself, try and find a specific story that proves the statement to be true. Remember, a story is not a list, so I don't want twelve short examples of how you're afraid of commitment; I want one story in great detail that proves this.

> Be unpredictable,
> be real, be interesting.
> Tell a good story.
>
> **—JAMES DASHNER,**
> **author, in** *Writer's Digest*

Here's a good formula for this style of storytelling (using a true story from my life):

1. Thesis statement: *I am the world's biggest fan of game shows—specifically,* The Price Is Right.

2. A little intro citing an example or two that exemplifies this: *As a kid, it was banned from my house. My father, an academic, told me, "That's a show for stupid people. We watch* Jeopardy! *in this house." So I used to sneak off and watch* The Price Is Right *like it was porn.*

3. Then I go into the meat of my story, which has a beginning, a middle, and an end, and builds to a climax. (I'm not going to write the whole story out here, but I'll give you a little taste.): *A few years ago, my husband and I* *visited Los Angeles, and the only goal I had for the trip was to become a contestant on* The Price Is Right. *I researched everything I could about how to get picked out of the audience at a taping. There was no way I was going to spend a day watching others play the greatest game ever invented. I am no spectator.*

At this point, I will recount the experience I had on the set of *The Price Is Right*, seen through the eyes of the world's biggest fan, as I declared I was in my thesis. At the end of my story, my intention is for you to believe I *am* the world's biggest fan of the show *The Price Is Right*, because I told a story that proved it.

Funny Teaching Anecdote: I used to always do this exercise in my classes using "Make a thesis statement about your love/sex/dating life, then tell a story that proves it." Then one day, I taught a class in which *3 out of 10* of the students were currently going through a divorce. I had no idea until I watched them one by one get up and say things like, "My thesis statement on love is 'I thought everything was fine, but I guess it wasn't'" and "I never thought he was going to leave me." And slowly I started to die in my chair. How was I supposed to know that 30 percent of the class was middivorce? Ever since then, I've opened the range of topics to other things.

PART 2

ELEMENTS OF A STORY

CHAPTER 6
PASSION

Emotion is contagious.

—MALCOLM GLADWELL,
The Tipping Point

———————————

I'm not a fan of Sarah Palin. However, I once had a student who grew up in the same town as her and thought of Sarah Palin as an honorary aunt. This student told a story—with passion, enthusiasm, and humor—about her fun "Auntie Sarah." For the five minutes that my student spoke, I genuinely liked Sarah Palin. Did the storyteller forever change my opinion of Sarah Palin? Absolutely not. After the story, I went right back to my original feelings.

It would take a lot more than a funny five-minute tale to change an opinion I feel that strongly about. But the storyteller did her job; she got me on board with her. She got me to listen and enjoy her story through her enthusiasm. I often think about this example when pondering how far passion can take you. If a person, via their passion, can get you to enjoy a story about a person you can't stand, then passion is a pretty valuable storytelling tool.

> *Indifference is the enemy of storytelling.*
> *If you don't feel strongly about what you*
> *are talking about, the audience won't care*
> *about it either.*

On the flip side, I don't care if you are telling me a story about having a gun pulled on you—if you don't seem to be affected by the events in your story, how can you expect anyone else to be?

Once you figure out things/people/foods/animals/ anything you are passionate about, it opens up a whole new world of stories to tell. You don't just have to tell stories about the wildest events of your life; you can tell stories about small things that you truly care about. So now the "crazy things never happen to me" excuse goes out the window.

> In general, don't portray any-
> thing that says "I'm too cool
> and I don't care."
>
> **—PAUL FEIG, director, author,
> creator of *Freaks and Geeks*, in
> *Los Angeles* magazine**

⌇ TELL YOUR STORY ⌇

Make a list of ten things you have a visceral reaction to.
Think of things/people/places that make you physically
react (positively or negatively). Maybe there's a specific
story in there!

~~~~~~~~~~~~~~~~~~~~~~~~~~~~

Here's an example of passion either killing or making a
story. When I was teaching once, a woman recounted her
journey of trying to have a baby, and all the steps she went
through to do so. In the end, she ended up not getting
pregnant. Now, most of us would agree that a decision to
bring a child into the world is a pretty big one, and trying
to make that happen would have some major stakes
involved. It's a life-changing decision. However, the student basically just told us the steps she went through, e.g.,
"Then when my boyfriend and I broke up, I tried artificial

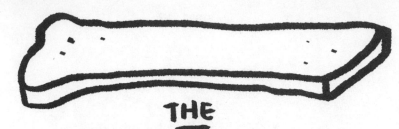

THE

PERSON WHO CAN KEEP US ON THE EDGE OF OUR SEATS WHILE TALKING ABOUT A TURKEY SANDWICH IS A TRULY GIFTED STORYTELLER

insemination, and that cost a lot of money. And when that didn't work, I tried in vitro fertilization, which was even more expensive. And then . . ." She gave us a full play-by-play, but she never reacted to what was happening. I didn't have a clue about how she felt concerning all she'd had to endure.

I asked her, "Well, did you want to have a baby? How badly?" And she replied, "Well, I kind of felt like if it happened, it happened, but if it didn't, it wasn't meant to be." While we've all had feelings of ambivalence in life, you can't expect to end up with a magnetic story if you're ambivalent about the topic. Without passion, her story fell flat. She didn't care, so we didn't. I ended up working with her on a different piece, about dating, which may on the surface seem less important, but she genuinely cared about what transpired. And the final story she showcased was wonderful.

> *As listeners, we often care more about how you felt about what happened than what actually happened.* *

---

* This principle is so important I really encourage you to write it down in a place that you will see it often.

Here's the other side of the coin. Another student, a middle-aged mother of three who worked at Verizon, came into class one day and told a story about baking cookies for the office Christmas party. Sounds kind of boring, right? Wrong. It was one of the funniest stories I have ever heard in my life, and I have heard a lot of stories. She talked about how she baked fortune cookies from scratch and wrote her own personalized fortunes inside, matching the font of actual fortune cookies. She got so into it she believed this Christmas party would launch her out of her miserable job at Verizon and into a new career of making personalized fortune cookies for weddings, graduations, office events, and more. No longer would she be stuck listening to people complain about their cellular reception. She would be a successful business owner, making her own hours and jetting off to tropical vacations whenever she pleased.

What actually happened was she arrived at the office Christmas party, proudly carrying her tray of cookies. Someone offhandedly said, "Put them over there," and they were placed in the back corner of the party, where they proceeded to fall apart over the course of the evening and be eaten by no one. While her coworkers scarfed down designer cupcakes, mini gingerbread houses, and eggnog brownies, my student pondered her life decisions. She said she was so crushed that the next day when her alarm went off, she couldn't get out of bed. "I would not be starting my fortune cookie business," she said. "I would not be jetting off to Aruba. I would instead be stuck answering phones at Verizon for the rest of my damn life."

The entire class was in stitches, some of us crying from laughter. This was a story about baking cookies for an office Christmas party. It was not about a life-changing event, like having a baby. But she cared so much—so much, in fact, that she couldn't get out of bed the next day. And we all cared right along with her. To this day, the Christmas cookie story remains one of my favorites of all time. The teller's passion was so contagious I still remember it vividly all these years later.

> *Feeling strongly towards or against some-thing/someone can make your story soar.*

Stories filled with negative passion can also really soar. I'm not saying that you should tell a story about how you just read a book about the dreadful prison conditions in America and you'd like to share with us a few highlights.*

---

* There is a time and a place for a speech like that, but it definitely isn't storytelling.

I'm saying that feeling passionately opposed to something can be quite amusing.

> I hate people who wear top hats, they look like assholes.
>
> **—JOHN WATERS,**
> **director, in *Salon* magazine**

Director John Waters's book *Role Models** contains a lot of intentionally funny musings, but none that made me laugh out loud more than his staunch opinions of grown men in top hats and cloaks. That Waters feels so strongly against something so silly makes for pure, ridiculous magic that I love to laugh at. Here are some other strong negative opinions I find stupid and/or hilarious:

- Elaine from *Seinfeld*'s absolute disgust for the film *The English Patient*
- The sincere hatred The Dude has for the Eagles in *The Big Lebowski*
- Barack Obama's referral to Kanye West as a "jackass"
- My husband's complete disdain for any chat/instant-message function, and his annoyance whenever anyone tries to message him. I laugh every time he passionately says "Everyone knows by now, I don't chat."

---

* Where a longer version of his *Salon* piece can be found.

⋛ TELL YOUR STORY ⋚

Fill in the blanks to figure out things you are passionate
about. Don't overthink it, and do not make a list of possible
answers. Instead, make a strong choice and stand by it.

I GET OVERLY EXCITED BY _____.

I PRETEND TO CARE ABOUT _____,
BUT I REALLY DON'T.

I PRETEND I DON'T CARE ABOUT _____,
BUT I REALLY DO.

I WORRY PEOPLE WILL FIND OUT _____.

~~~~~~~~~~~~~~~~~~~~~~~~~~~~~

One more thing: try to be a little creative. These are a few
unoriginal responses that I hear all the time:

"I don't understand what the big deal is about marriage/
weddings/ children/the Kardashians." (No one understands what the big deal is about the Kardashians!)

"I pretend to care about your kids/the environment/pol-
itics, but I really don't."

"I pretend I don't care about what other people think of
me/my weight, but I really do."

Here are some answers that inspired some amazing stories:

I GET OVERLY EXCITED BY MINIATURE SCALE MODELS OF LARGE THINGS.

I PRETEND TO CARE ABOUT BANKING, BUT I REALLY DON'T.*

I PRETEND I DON'T CARE ABOUT ROMANTIC COMEDIES, BUT I REALLY DO.

I WORRY PEOPLE WILL FIND OUT THAT I AM NOT REALLY FROM SPAIN.

~~~~~~~~~~~~~~~~

When it comes to passion, sometimes you can go too far. If you ever watch the show *Shark Tank*, a show where entrepreneurs present inventions to millionaire and billionaire investors, you know that each episode usually features someone both closing a deal and killing a deal—all because of their use/misuse of passion.

---

*   A banker at the executive level said this, and a very funny story came of it.

TIP: Passion is your enemy when . . .

1. You are crying, not just tearing up but sobbing uncontrollably during your story.

2. You are screaming at your audience to get them to see your point.

3. You are laughing at your own jokes, not genuinely but uncomfortably, in order to signal to your audience "Isn't this funny?"

4. You tell your listeners how they should be feeling, e.g., "Guys, this is supposed to be funny" or "Why aren't you on my side here?"

Countless entrepreneurs on *Shark Tank* say things like "I think this is important. It can change our lives. You should see how important this is." But that's not the way to get a person on board. The investors either feel your genuine passion and share it, or they don't. No one likes being told how to feel. We feel things organically, or we don't. Some people wept uncontrollably at the end of *The Notebook*. Some of us (like me) changed the channel midway through the movie, because we just didn't get what the big deal was.

> *Don't alienate your audience by abusing passion.*

⟩ TELL YOUR STORY ⟨

Emotion is both an enemy and an ally in storytelling. Let's do another fill-in-the-blank exercise to see what really gets you going.

_____ MAKES ME CRY.

_____ MAKES ME SO ANGRY.

I CAN'T BELIEVE THE WAY I ONCE REACTED TO _____.

_____ IS HOW I LEARNED I HATED _____.

~~~~~~~~~~~~~~~~~~~~~~~~~~

When doing this exercise, try to think of the dumbest thing in the world that makes you cry. For me, that answer would be "sappy movies on airplanes."*

The object of figuring out what makes you cry is not to tell the story of the most horrific thing you can think of but to find the humor in heightened emotion. The same goes for the "angry" fill-in-the-blank. Sure, injustice/abuse/corruption/etc. makes us all angry. But what about

---

* I recently sobbed like a baby on a cross-country flight while watching some Vince Vaughn romantic comedy that wasn't even sad.

the dumb stuff that really sets you off? What's a silly pet peeve of yours? For me, it's guys walking down the street with parrots on their shoulders. You are not a pirate! West Seventy-Second Street is not a natural habitat for a tropical bird! And don't give me a look to say, "What are you looking at?" when I stare a little longer at you because you have a goddamn parrot on your shoulder! Also, I'm not saying we're superior here, but I'd just like to say that I have never seen a woman walking down the street with a parrot on her shoulder.

> Every moment in life is a learning experience. Or what good is it, right?
>
> **—PAUL, in John Guare's *Six Degrees of Separation***

For the second-to-last fill-in-the-blank, think specifically. Don't answer with "I can't believe the way I once reacted to people's differences." That's way too vague. A student once answered, "I can't believe the way I once reacted to my luggage being lost at Newark Airport," and then proceeded to go into a hilarious story, ending in her publicly humiliating herself.

With the last prompt, challenge yourself to tell a story in one sentence. Hands down, the best answer I ever got to this prompt was from the shyest student in the world. She stood up and quietly said in front of the entire class, "Anal sex is how I learned I hated anal sex." And then the entire class erupted into laughter—a loud belly laugh that went on for minutes. She told the whole story in ten words.

So now that you get the concept of passion driving a story—strong passion both for and against something—I have another exercise for you.

⋛ TELL YOUR STORY ⋛

I call this "The Moment When You Lost It." Think of a time you snapped—and I mean really snapped. Don't say to yourself, "I am really even-keeled. I never lose it." I call bullshit on that. Everyone has lost it sometime. Okay, so maybe you didn't behave like Michael Douglas's character William "D-Fens" Foster in *Falling Down*.* But you've certainly lost your cool at some point. Recount the story, and when you do, try to find the humor in it.

---

* A classic '90s movie where Douglas has an unbearably frustrating day in Los Angeles and reaches his boiling point, which causes him to acquire weapons and go on a shooting rampage.

One is tempted to define man as a rational animal who always loses his temper when he is called upon to act in accordance with the dictates of reason.

—**OSCAR WILDE,**
The Artist as Critic

IF YOU CAN LAUGH NOW ABOUT THE LAST TIME YOU "LOST IT," CHANCES ARE YOUR AUDIENCE WILL FIND IT FUNNY TOO

CHAPTER 7

LAYERING A STORY

The moral of Pete's story is: No matter
what you step in, keep walking along
and singing your song... because it's all good.

—*PETE THE CAT:*
I LOVE MY WHITE SHOES by Eric Litwin

My two-year-old son loves the Pete the Cat children's
book series, about what I believe to be a total stoner
cat. Pete has many adventures while learning to be chill
and not get upset over the little problems in life, such as
stepping in a pile of blueberries, having all four buttons
of his favorite yellow shirt pop off one by one, and having
to fill in last-minute for stoner cat Santa, who has a cold.

THERE IS ABSOLUTELY NO NEED TO TELL US THE MORAL OF YOUR STORY.
WE GET IT

Often at the end of these books, the author will blatantly tell us the moral of the story, usually something about remembering to be superchill. This is because these books are geared toward children, who often need the message of the story spelled out for them word for word. My son does not understand subtext or metaphors or subtlety. Adults, however, usually do.

> I have no idea to this day what those two Italian ladies were singing about. Truth is, I don't want to know. Some things are best left unsaid. I'd like to think they were singing about something so beautiful, it can't be expressed in words, and makes your heart ache because of it.
>
> **—RED (played by Morgan Freeman),**
> *The Shawshank Redemption*

When trying to convey a deeper message within a true story, the best storytellers sneak it in without being too heavy-handed. Otherwise, you risk coming off as preachy or sappy. David Sedaris is a master of this. A great example is his *New Yorker* essay "Now We Are Five," about his sister's suicide. It's one of his darkest pieces, yet I have seen him perform it live and it still has levity and laugh-out-loud moments. It's worth the read.

> ### PHRASES THAT MAKE ME GAG WHEN HEARING PEOPLE TELL STORIES:
>
> - And then it hit me.
> - And that's when I realized ...
> - And then it happened.
> - And now I know ...
> - My point is ...
> - The moral of the story is ...
> - So, what I learned was ...
> - The takeaway is ...

Toward the end of the movie *The Wizard of Oz*, Dorothy says, "There's no place like home" several times. Most people would say that's the intended moral of the story. However, another popular theory is that the story is an allegory for the changing American monetary policy at the beginning of the twentieth century. There are some other theories floating around (religious allegory, feminist allegory, and many more), but the most common consensus is that the yellow brick road symbolizes the gold standard, the green Emerald City represents the dollar, and so on.*

So let's say this *Wizard of Oz* theory is accurate. At no point in the movie does Dorothy look to camera, break the fourth wall, and say, "Hey, guys, I know you're all thinking this movie is all about my journey back home to Kansas, yadda yadda yadda, but really, my point is the Populist Movement really went to shit at the turn of century." The film speaks for itself. And we all take *something* from the film, even if we don't get the exact point intended.

Sure, there are exceptions to this. There are exceptions to most things in life. In a famous interview, comedian Dave Chappelle told journalist Anderson Cooper that one of the reasons he walked from his sketch comedy show on Comedy Central was because a portion of the audience might be "laughing for the wrong reasons." This is an understandable concern, considering how much *Chappelle's Show* did with the touchy subject of race. And there was no way he could stop and say, "Are you laughing *with* me or *at* me?" From what I gathered from his interview with Cooper, it seems he got worried that people were missing his point and that unintentional damage could be done to race relations.

---

* Feel free to go down a Google rabbit hole on this; you'll find endless articles written about it.

WHAT'S IMPORTANT IS THAT YOUR STORY MOVES US IN *SOME* WAY. DON'T GET CAUGHT UP IN MAKING SURE WE SEE *YOUR* POINT.

But Chappelle was performing in front of a much wider audience than you can expect to be telling a story for. Therefore, there is no reason to stop anywhere within your piece to tell us your point. You are not reading a children's story to a toddler; you are recounting a true-life story to adults.

Q: So how am I supposed to get a deeper message across without sounding preachy, sappy, or pretentious?

A: Well, have you ever heard someone say, "What's your motivation?" when talking about acting? What I mean is, often when actors are doing a scene, they will try to figure out why the characters they're playing are acting a certain way, i.e. the characters' "motivation." So if the scene is a couple drinking coffee, one actor might use having just come back from having an affair as motivation for the scene. This actor might do subtle things in his scene to convey that he is hiding something, or distracted, or overcompensating. His motivation won't be revealed to the audience, but the performer knows it, and it drives his acting. Without the actor knowing his motivation, the scene could read simply as two people drinking coffee and talking about their day.

We can apply this same principle to storytelling. Your point, or moral, or deeper message, should be known to you, to drive the writing and telling of your tale, but in my opinion, you should keep it to yourself. Just like in the coffee scene, the actor harboring the secret that he just returned from having an affair never stops the scene to say, "By the way, I know you think I'm talking about coffee, but actually I am falling out of love with you and in love with someone else. So when I say, 'Do you want your coffee black, like usual?' really I mean I'm bored with you." Later, the audience may put the pieces together, or not.

Whatever your universal theme is, you should be able to explain it to yourself in just a few words. It's your secret weapon when you tell your story. You never need to reveal it. Have you ever been to a yoga class where the teacher asks you to set your intention at the start? It's something you silently keep to yourself but let drive your actions. The same goes for the universal theme of your story.

> *Trick your audience into hearing your bigger message by layering it into your story. Don't beat us over the head with it. Write it at the top of your story script and let it be just for you.*

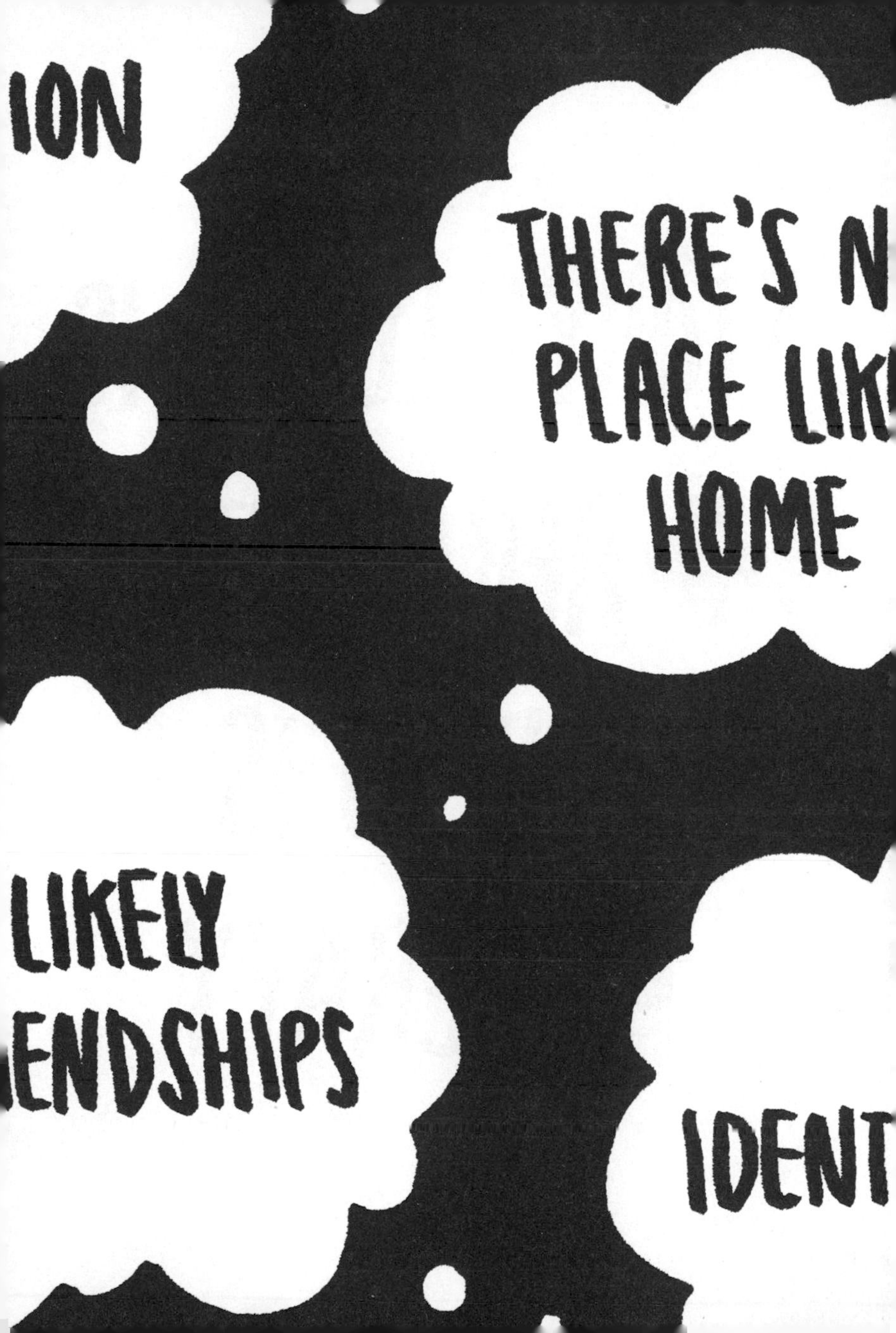
ION
THERE'S N
PLACE LIK
HOME
LIKELY
ENDSHIPS
IDENT

STORYTELLING IS
✚HERAPEUTIC,
BUT SO IS
✚HERAPY

Remember, it's not crucial that your audience gets *your* point, just that they get *a* point. Above all, what really matters is that you entertain, move, and affect them. Storytelling isn't therapy or a political platform. There are plenty of therapists and political rallies you can go to. Yes, storytelling is therapeutic. Many times I have felt better about a life event after a roomful of people have laughed at my misfortunes, but I wouldn't use the time I get to tell stories to spread a political message. That would feel like I was abusing the privilege.

I'm going to be blunt here. You know when someone says to you, "I had the craziest dream last night—let me tell you all about it" and you'd rather gouge your eyes out than be stuck listening to it? Cut to twenty minutes later and they're still going on saying things like, "And when the magic cauliflower spoke, I realized it was my dad, telling me it's okay to move on." The same goes for heavy-handed storytelling about some realization you had. I know you care that the puppy in your dream is you, and the dream means you need to be more of a risk taker, and if the puppy can get back up on its feet, maybe you can too and maybe you *will* find love again, and that's your point. But long-winded self-realizations can drag when telling a story. The audience doesn't care about all that. What we *do* care about is the disastrous relationship you had (feel free to leave out the puppy), because we can relate to that. Maybe I will take "Know when to get out" as your message. Perhaps another will take "We all make bad decisions when we are in love" as your point. Who cares? We both liked your story, were affected by it, and were entertained.

≷ TELL YOUR STORY ≷

Think of a small moment in your life that actually turned out to be much bigger. For example, you couldn't afford your dream school, so instead you went to a community college, and that's where you met your wife. Trick us into hearing a bigger point by telling what at first seems like a relatively small story (not having enough money for college), and turning it into a big story (finding true love).

My friend and co-host for *Stripped Stories* Giulia Rozzi tells a wonderfully layered story that took home the grand prize at the Moth GrandSLAM storytelling competition. It's a laugh-out-loud story all the way through about singing with a live band backing her up and finally feeling like the rock star she always knew she was. She takes us through the utter joy she has singing, and then she walks us through the moment when she steps offstage and cries to her friends immediately, "I want a divorce." This is the perfect example of a carefully layered story. We think it's a fun recounting of a memorable night out, but in fact it symbolizes the entire demise of her marriage. Slowly we realize, that this moment singing is the first time she's felt like herself all year and how much of a release it was for her. The other way to tell this tale would be to walk us through the death of her relationship step by painful step, repeatedly saying, "This wasn't meant to be." One version is therapy. Giulia's version is storytelling.

> I have so many opinions about everything it just comes out during my music. It's a battle for me. I try not to be preachy. That's a real danger.
>
> **—NEIL YOUNG, musician**

I think a lot of heavy-handed storytelling comes from lack of self-confidence. The storyteller doesn't trust that his/her story is "working," so often he/she will really force the point. Personally, I watched about four seasons of the TV show *House M.D.* before noticing that Dr. House was inspired by Sherlock Holmes, and Dr. Wilson was Watson. I mean, their names are even derived from Holmes and Watson! But I enjoyed the program nonetheless. Actually, I didn't even enjoy the show any more after I discovered the creator's intention.

I also believe forcing a point on an audience comes down to control. You can't control whether or not someone will get your point or find something funny. Sometimes things go over our heads. Sometimes we get it. Sometimes we don't. Sometimes we're dealing with our own issues and want to take a certain meaning from a tale that applies to our current situation. *Let go of the desire to control the audience.*

Musicians have really nailed the concept of letting a song's message speak for itself. Many hit songs have snuck by us without anyone realizing what they were really intended to be about. And if these songs had been less subtle in their message, they may have never made it to the radio in the first place.

• "Born in the U.S.A." by Bruce Springsteen—*This is not an "I Love America" anthem. It's about a working-class man coming back from Vietnam and being shunned by his own country.*

• Madonna's "Material Girl" (written by Peter Brown and Robert Rans)—*This song is not all about how much girls should pursue rich men, but instead about wanting to date*

TRYING TO CONTROL AN AUDIENCE'S REACTION IS ESSENTIALLY TRYING TO CONTROL THEIR FEELINGS, AND THAT'S IMPOSSIBLE *a man who has his own thing going on so the woman doesn't have to devote constant attention to him. But they cleverly disguised this in the iconic video, didn't they?*

• "Every Breath You Take" by the Police (written by Sting)—*This is not a sweet love song about always being there for someone, but instead a dark look at a possessive lover's thoughts.*

• "Semi-Charmed Life" by Third Eye Blind—*This song is about a man and woman on a meth binge. Let it be known that in college, I was involved in a show in which a catchy, smiley tap dance was performed to this song. A song about meth!*

So think of the subtlety of music when composing a story with a greater point. It's fine to have a bigger point. Just let it come through on its own.

> The more efficient a force is, the more silent and the more subtle it is.
> **—MAHATMA GANDHI**

CHAPTER 8

PERSPECTIVE

My mother wanted us to
understand that the tragedies
of your life one day have the potential
to be comic stories the next.

**—NORA EPHRON,
journalist, screenwriter, and director**

We often tell others going through a rough time, "Someday this will make a great story." I am from the school of thought that the darker a situation, the better story it will eventually make.

Spalding Gray was an actor who became a pioneer in what he called "autobiographical monologues," which were lengthy true stories from his life told directly to his audience. Gray would sit at a table and speak, with his trademark glass of water as his only prop. He hit mainstream success in the '80s, and I will be referencing him quite a bit throughout the rest of this book, as he is the closest thing we have to a founding father of theatrical storytelling.

Spalding Gray struggled when life was pleasant (for more on this, read his book *Morning, Noon and Night*), as he often felt uninspired during these periods. Gray said most of his monologues were "based on crisis." I think he would have agreed with me that life can be broken down into two categories: a good time or a good story.

Some of the greatest stories ever told stem from what would seem like the least funny events.

• Nora Ephron wrote the semiautobiographical novel *Heartburn* after her husband, Carl Bernstein, had an affair and their marriage dissolved. She then turned it into a movie starring a couple of actors you may have heard of: Jack Nicholson and Meryl Streep.

• Spalding Gray's monologue *Gray's Anatomy* was written about a rare eye disease he had. Instead of recounting his experience in medical jargon, Gray takes us on a seriocomic journey of his quest for answers. This monologue became a Steven Soderbergh–directed movie and a published book.*

---

* Not to be confused with McDreamy's *Grey's Anatomy*, a television show I have never seen.

• David Sedaris wrote one of his most moving and iconic essays, "Repeat After Me," after backing out of a movie deal he had with director Wayne Wang, who was already casting the movie he was making based on Sedaris's stories. This was an almost disaster turned brilliant story, which then was published in the best-selling book *Dress Your Family in Corduroy and Denim*.

I guarantee you, getting cheated on, partially losing your eyesight, and making a possibly career-killing decision would not be funny to you at the time. So how do we make compelling stories out of these unfortunate events?

STEPS TO TAKING LIFE'S MISHAPS & MAKING THEM INTO STORY MAGIC

1. Let time pass between the event and talking about the event.

I can't tell you the exact amount of time you need to wait to talk about something that upset you. There is no formula. This past week I told a story onstage about something that happened two nights before. I was already laughing about it. On the flip side, I have never talked onstage about one relationship I had in my early twenties. Despite many years passing, I just don't find anything funny about that relationship or its demise. So I choose not to tell that story.

Can you recount the tale without having a strong physical reaction, such as shaking, heart racing, switching to your "angry voice," or crying? (I'm not talking about getting a little teary-eyed here; I mean full-force black-eye-makeup-running-down-the-face crying.) If you can, then enough time has passed. If you now find what once seemed like a tragedy actually kind of humorous, go for it!

2. Have you moved on?

You need to be over the situation, not knee-deep in it. Really think about it. I once saw Guns N' Roses bassist Duff McKagan tell a story about almost dying from drug and alcohol use, and how he restarted his life to become something he never imagined it could be. He was clearly over it—sober for decades and happily married with two kids. If he had tried to tell the story of being addicted to drugs while still struggling with the problem, the story would have been more like, "I did this risky thing, then this crazy thing, then I almost died, and now we'll see." He wouldn't have been sure he could make it in this world sober. He wouldn't have known what was next. Now, McKagan can reflect on his drug years as a separate part of his life. He has moved on.

3. Is it actually over?

Are you in the process of switching careers from lawyer to pottery shop owner? Hearing the story of how you hate law and how now you're considering opening a pottery shop but you aren't sure how to make that happen and you're currently broke is likely to leave your audience feeling unsatisfied. There is no ending to this tale. We want to hear the story of how you walked away from an unfulfilling career in law and successfully transitioned to a less lucrative but more fulfilling job. We want to be inspired because you figured it out on your own, not concerned about whether or not you're going to be okay. There should be some closure to the situation.

4. Are you able to take a step back and see what that life event was *really* about?

What was *really* going on at the point of your story? Here's an example:

When I first moved to Los Angeles, I was pursuing acting. I'd had some success professionally in New York, and I figured it would be an easy transition. Instead, I went to an LA acting class, where I was removed from the group by the teacher to be told privately that I was "fat." Humiliated, I then went on a strict no-carb diet, which caused me to order steak skewers at a restaurant a few nights later, where I proceeded to choke on the steak. I was then Heimliched by a nice guy, which took three tries, and I truly believed I was going to die between the second and third. Then the guy who Heimliched me told me he was a distant relative of Dr. Heimlich, and he had been waiting his entire life for this moment.

None of this would have happened if the acting teacher hadn't called me fat. I would have ordered a large serving of fried calamari as usual and not choked. Later, this choking incident became a sign to me that pursuing acting in LA was maybe not for me. However, while the steak was lodged in my esophagus, I certainly could not see the bigger picture. The next day, with a sore rib cage and a sudden fear of beef products, I still couldn't see the bigger picture. I needed to take a step back and process the series of events, which now seem hilarious.

QUIZ: SHOULD YOU TELL THIS STORY?

1. You just got diagnosed with testicular cancer. The doctors are optimistic because you caught it early and it's treatable in 99.2 percent of patients. This is by far the hardest thing you have gone through yet, and the support of your family and friends is so moving you want to talk about it.

☐ YES   ☐ NO

Answer: No.

Why? Because I said, "You *just* got diagnosed with testicular cancer." You are at the beginning of a story; it is far from over. You are going through something, not reflecting back on it. Also, it will be hard to keep emotion under control while recounting this tale. Wait on this.

Some of you readers may be thinking, "But what about comedian Tig Notaro's now-famous stand-up set from August 2012 about just losing her mother, enduring a breakup, and getting diagnosed with breast cancer all at the same time? She found out just days before that she had cancer and the set was still entertaining."

My response is, surely there are exceptions to everything I say in this book. Just remember they are exceptions, not the norm. Also remember, at the time of this set, Tig Notaro had been performing stand-up comedy for many years. She was a pro. I don't recommend taking a risk like this in the beginning stages.

~~~~~~~~~~~~~~~~~~~~~~~~

2. Your job as a personal assistant to the Wicked Witch of the Northwest has been driving you crazy. You have many examples of why working for this woman is a nightmare, but yesterday her insistence that you carry her luggage while she did a phone session with her therapist in front of you was the final straw. You quit!

☐ YES   ☐ NO

Answer: Yes.

That's my vote. It sounds like this story has a beginning, a middle, and an end. The job probably started out okay, then warning signs kept appearing, finally building to the final straw. You most likely feel great about this choice, and know that whatever's next can't be worse, so I think you would leave an audience inspired and with a sense of closure. Even though only a day has passed, you are already laughing at the experience.

~~~~~~~~~~~~~~~~~~~~~~~~

3. Your wedding was a disaster. It's been three years since the big day, and yet the memories of friends letting you down, selfish relatives, and regretful overspending are still fresh in your mind. There's a great story in there, and it's been three years, so maybe it's time to tell it.

☐ YES ☐ NO

Answer: No.

Yes, three years have passed, but it sounds like you aren't over it yet. This story could turn out to be a rant, and too much complaining might turn people off.

Yesterday's weirdness is
tomorrow's reason why.
—HUNTER S. THOMPSON,
The Curse of Lono,
journalist and author

Another aspect of perspective is what many people refer
to as "voice." It's your view on a situation that makes it
unique and interesting, not the situation itself.

⋛ TELL YOUR STORY ⋚

Something I have recently started doing in classes (and I
suggest you try this the next time you are out with a group
of people) is to fill in the end of this sentence:

I WAS HOT AND THIRSTY, THE PERSON STANDING NEXT
TO ME IN LINE OFFERED ME A SIP OF HIS WATER,
AND I THOUGHT _____.

I just did this exercise in a class, and the answers ranged
from "Why is this person trying to poison me?" to "What
a nice person! Thank you!" An individual's reaction to this

tells so much about who they are. The person who thinks
they are being poisoned has a much more jaded view
of the world than the person who thinks a kind stranger
is helping them out. However, we would never know that
either of these people was jaded or wide-eyed if they didn't
inform us of their perspective on the situation. Without
perspective, the story becomes simply, *I was hot and
thirsty, and the stranger standing next to me in line offered
me a sip of his water.*

> "Do the other kids make fun of
> you? For how you talk?"
>
> "Sometimes."
>
> "So why don't you do something
> about it? You could learn to talk
> differently, you know."
>
> "But this is my voice. How
> would you be able to tell when I
> was talking?"
>
> —*Before I Fall* by LAUREN OLIVER

I will never forget the adorable recent college grad from
Staten Island who took classes from me in New York City.
In one particular story, she recounted the tale of a bad

IT'S NOT JUST THE EVENTS IN YOUR STORY THAT MAKE IT ENTERTAINING; IT'S YOUR REACTION TO THE EVENTS date. It wasn't so disastrous that it was like a scene in *The 40 Year-Old Virgin*, but just kind of meh. The story was dragging a bit until she said in her thick Staten Island accent, "And then at dinner he started axing me awl about myself . . . and I don't like that." The class howled, myself included. Excuse my broad judgment here, but what woman doesn't like talking about herself? Specifically, what woman on a date with a man wouldn't want him to seem interested in her life? Isn't that what most people are looking for—someone who listens to us and asks us about our days? The fact that this student had no interest in talking about herself gave such a unique perspective that it drove what was a fairly uninteresting story into a suddenly hysterical story.

Another thing I like to do when telling a story is think about who I was at the time. This is hard, I know, but try to take away the adult/mature perspective that you surely have now (what, you still don't consider yourself a mature adult?) and think about how you might have reacted then.

In my story "A Very Tiny Grownup," I am twelve years old, recounting an interaction with a thirty-year-old bank teller, in which I say he spends his off time "counting piles of fresh money." I obviously know now that bank tellers aren't filthy rich people with mountains of cash to rival Scrooge McDuck. But at twelve, I thought that bank tellers got to keep a lot of the money they dealt with at their counter.*

Take yourself back to your thoughts at the time of your story: Where was your self-esteem? Were you overconfident in a way that seems really juvenile now? Were you insecure and scared of the world? Think of job interviews you've had in your life. Were you so cocky and inexperienced at the time that you thought you nailed something that in hindsight you realize you totally bombed? These perspectives can add so much to a story.

⋛ TELL YOUR STORY ⋜

Write out your morning routine.

Even if you are not a person of routine (e.g., a freelancer rather than a person who reports to the same job every day), there are still things you do every morning such as drink coffee, check e-mail, etc.

---

* In New Jersey, where I grew up, a gas station attendant pumps your gas for you. Back then, each attendant would have a giant wad of cash they would take out every time you paid to make change. I believed that was all theirs to keep and that those gas station attendants were the wealthiest people in the world.

~~~~~~~~~~~~~~~~~~~~~~~~~

For me, it looks something like this:

6:45 My son wakes me up, crying "Mommy" from his room.

6:47 I go get him out of his crib and put him on the potty.

7:01 We go to the bedroom to say hi to Daddy and the dog.

7:01 We lounge in bed together as a family.

7:15 My husband takes the dog out. I go to the kitchen with my son, where I feed the fish, feed the dog, and make my son breakfast.

~~~~~~~~~~~~~~~~~~~~~~~~~

This is tedious to write and surely for you to read. Now, write out your morning routine with perspective/reactions to everything that happens. I want to know your thoughts/inner monologue about it all. Here's mine:

6:45 I'm fast asleep when my son starts crying for Mommy. Why is it he never asks for Daddy? I stay still, not moving, hoping my husband will offer to go in there so I can get an extra five minutes of sleep. Nope, my husband is snoring happily; he doesn't even hear our son. I wish I were that person, out as soon as I hit the pillow, sleeping through anything. But no, I am a light sleeper, who can only sleep in a bed, never even on an airplane, despite the over-twenty-four-hour flight I took to Australia once. Oh, he's really crying now—I need to get in there.

6:47 I go into my son's room. I am such a jerk. He's so cute, and so happy to see me. He looks adorable with his hair tousled like that. I should have come in sooner. Fail. Okay, we're off to the potty. Please don't let him ask me to watch *Yo Gabba Gabba!* while you're trying to pee. The songs get stuck in my head and stay there, and that's half the reason I have trouble sleeping. Do you even understand how hard it is to drift off while "Party in My Tummy" plays on a loop in your head? Score! He actually peed in the potty. I still am amazed that we successfully potty trained this toddler. That's it, right? That's the last big hurdle of parenting? Please tell me it's the last big hurdle of parenting. He's only two, and I'm already spent.

~~~~~~~~~~~~~~~~~~~~~~~~~~~~~~~

I could go on and on, but you get the point. What was a boring recitation of events has now become the seedling of a story. Or at the least you feel like you know a little more about who I am due to my perspective on ordinary events.

Another person might write this version of the same events:

6:45 I'm woken up by my son crying, "Mommy!" I jump out of bed to see if he's okay. Whew! He didn't die in his sleep. When will I stop worrying about this? It's been two years.

6:47 I get him out of the crib and to the potty. I'm still waiting for him to pee there. I don't know if I did the potty-training method right. The book said he would get it in forty-eight hours, but it's been two weeks. Okay, he went. Maybe he just needed a second. Remember to read in the book about delayed peeing. On second thought, I might need to read a second book on potty training.

~~~~~~~~~~~~~~~~~~~~~~~~~~~~

As you can see, the second person is a little higher-strung than I am when it comes to parenting. However, if we both just recounted events without giving them a personal voice, you might never know how different our personalities are.

> Screen acting is reacting.
> —**JOHN WAYNE, actor***

---

* Well, Mr. Wayne, so is storytelling!

CHAPTER 9
CHARACTER

If I continued to stand here,
looking at the audience.
What might I say?

—SPALDING GRAY*

Spalding Gray wrote the above question in his journal
in 1972, before he ventured into what we now call storytelling. I just love the idea of him standing onstage as a
character in a play, wondering if it would be possible to
stand in front of an audience just as himself, and whether

---

* On his director's instruction to drop his character at the end of
his soliloquy in *The Tooth of Crime* and just stand there looking at
the audience.

or not that would be interesting. I bet you're wondering the same thing.*

Q: If I stood before my boardroom/college alumni association/church retreat/etc. and spoke simply as myself, would I be interesting enough to hold their attention?

A: Yes. But first, let's identify who you are as a character. Let's dive into the specific traits that make you, well . . . you. You'll want to take your endearing traits and use them to your advantage. You might want to acknowledge anything that is obvious about you right away, so as not to distract from your story. Then move on.

For example, I once broke my foot, shattering the bone, by dropping a bottle of Bud Light on it at a precarious angle. It should be noted that I hate beer and find Bud Light disgusting, and I wasn't even drinking when it happened. I broke my foot simply *carrying* a Bud Light from one spot in the room to the other. That being said, I had a cast up to my knee that was very distracting when I performed. I simply would say at the top of each live story,

---

* It certainly was interesting enough. Gray won an Obie Award and a Guggenheim Fellowship for his autobiographical monologue *Swimming to Cambodia*, which eventually became a film directed by future Academy Award–winning director Jonathan Demme.

"I broke my foot, the cast comes off in six weeks, and I'll be fine. Anyway . . ." People were able to focus on my stories rather than my foot after that.

On the flip side, I was once at the Moth StorySLAM in Brooklyn, an open-mic storytelling competition when a short guy wearing glasses and a pink-and-brown argyle sweater got up to tell his story. He couldn't have looked less tough, but when he opened his mouth, he had a raspy, gravelly deep voice like Kiefer Sutherland's. Then he dove into a story about his days on a ranch. The entire audience, myself included, had this feeling of "What's going on? What we see doesn't match what we're hearing." A few storytellers later, a pale, gaunt-looking guy got up and began his story by saying, "I know I look like what you all think a vegetarian looks like, but I tried that for a while, and I'm done with it. And I know you think I look like a cancer patient, but I'm done with that too." After a big laugh, he went into a (can you believe it?) funny story about having cancer. And he won the competition.

The second storyteller worked with what his appearance already showed about him as a character and used it to his advantage. The first storyteller worked against what he already had going on. Had the argyle-sweater guy said something like this—"So I work in publishing now, obviously, because in what other field could I be considered edgy for wearing pink argyle, but before I moved to New York, I actually worked on a ranch"—the audience would have been much more on board after an intro like that.

～～～～～～～～～～～～～～～

A student of mine, named Danielle Perez*, who is a stand-up summed this concept up very well to me in a class I taught recently. She said, "Before I took your storytelling class, I felt like I had to spend my whole time onstage talking about how I was in a wheelchair, because that's the first thing everyone notices about me. It's not like I can completely ignore that I use a wheelchair in my material either. Now what I do is quickly acknowledge the chair, and then move on. It's working great, and now I am diving into what I really want to talk about."

Studies show that many of us tend to stereotype the people we encounter, even if we try not to.**

So think of storytelling in the constructs of social situations. You would probably get annoyed if *all* a friend talked about was being a woman, or being African American,

---

* The infamous *The Price Is Right* treadmill winner.
** For more on this, check out the book *Blindspot: Hidden Biases of Good People*, in which psychologists Mahzarin R. Banaji and Anthony G. Greenwald dive into hidden biases. This is based on their experiences with the Implicit Association Test, which you can take online.

or being a single parent, or being divorced, and so on. But if in ten years of friendship your friend never once acknowledged or spoke of his/her gender, race, family, or relationship situation, it might seem like your friendship was a little one-dimensional and impersonal. I'm not saying to begin every story with "So I'm a woman," or to tell twelve different stories exclusively about the struggles that come with being a woman. But if you're a woman and you're telling a story about your decision to become a police officer, it might be interesting to include the history of jobs the women in your family have had, especially if you come from a long line of housewives and stay-at-home moms. A female police officer who is pursuing the exact opposite of her family's traditional gender roles is a lot more interesting than simply "an aspiring police offer." By including your own spin on what people might be thinking, you're adding drama and taking charge of the running conclusions, often incorrect, that your audience is already subconsciously making.

Here's a good example of redirecting people's thoughts, then moving on to what you really want to talk about: I once got up on stage when I was eight and a half months pregnant, to tell a story that had nothing to do with being pregnant. If I didn't acknowledge this giant belly in front of me, the audience, whether they want to admit it or not, would have made a snap judgment about my situation. "She's about to burst. Why is she up there? Why isn't she resting?" or "She's so lucky; she's about to have a baby." Or "I wonder when her baby is due." I stepped onstage and said, "I just got off the phone with my mother before I came here. She said to me, 'You know, Margot, when I was eight months pregnant, that's when I started *losing* the baby weight.'" The audience groaned in sympathy with me. I continued, "So that's how my day's been going. And I'd really like to talk about anything besides being pregnant, so here goes . . ."

Had I spent my entire set talking about the pregnancy, it would have become tiresome. Had I not acknowledged it, it could have been a giant elephant in the room. So like the student mentioned previously said, I acknowledged it, then moved on.*

---

* It's now been two years since I had the baby, and I still haven't lost all the pregnancy weight. So I guess you're winning, Mom.

⋛ TELL YOUR STORY ⋛

This one is best done with a group that's meeting for the first time, as an icebreaker. Have everyone take a turn entering the room and just standing in front of the others for about thirty seconds. No talking/dancing/silly faces/ etc. allowed. The people seated should write down five very specific first impressions of the person standing before them—the more specific, the better. Stay away from broad, safe descriptions such as "nice" and don't write about people's bodies, e.g., "too skinny." Instead, write really specific guesses about them, like "drinks chamomile tea," "plays piano," or "never forgets a birthday." You will be shocked at how much we infer about a person in the first instant we see them.

~~~~~~~~~~~~~~~~~~~~~~

I do this exercise to show potential storytellers what their audience may be thinking about them already upon first glance. If everyone is thinking, "Looks like he played college football," and you, in fact, did, why not mention that somewhere in your story, even if your story is about parenting. For example, you could say, "I thought of my years getting slammed on that football field by college athletes and decided I was not going to lose this battle to my five-foot-tall fifteen-year-old daughter." That sentence explains so much more about where you are coming from in the argument you're describing than saying, "I was really struggling with this disagreement with my daughter." In the second sentence, we don't know who you are as a person; in the first one, we know you are a former college football player dealing with the trials and tribulations of teenage girls. You are a much clearer character by acknowledging what we all may be suspecting already.

> Doing sketch comedy on live television while pregnant is like wearing a sombrero. You can pretend to be a serious person, but the giant hat gives you away.
>
> **—AMY POEHLER, comedian***

---

* So you might as well acknowledge that sombrero!

⋛ TELL YOUR STORY ⋚

Think about a book, song, movie, or TV show that has
a character you strongly relate to, and try to figure out
specifically what makes you connect. So let's say you
have always felt a special kinship with Lloyd Dobler from
Say Anything. Try to find the clip that exemplifies the
quality of Lloyd that you like best. Study the specific clip
and isolate exactly why you see yourself in Lloyd.

~~~~~~~~~~~~~~~~~~~~~~~~~~~~~~~

Often when I do this exercise, students will choose a
clip or passage about a character that exemplifies what
they *want to be*. I have actually lost count of how many
times I have asked students, "Are you really a cowboy?"
or "So what is it about this Robert Redford character that
you truly identify with?" Or, my personal favorite, "How
exactly are you similar to Robert Redford playing a cowboy?" Look, we all want to be Robert Redford. But really
challenge yourself to find a character who is actually like
you. It might help to ask friends/family for suggestions. If
this exercise stumps you, try the next one.

⋛ TELL YOUR STORY ⋛

List three characters you relate to, and then list three characters you *want* to be like.

~~~~~~~~~~~~~~~~~~~~~~~~~~~~~~

The dichotomy is usually quite hilarious. It's something that can even be included when you tell a story. "I fancy myself a 'Rachel from *Friends*' type, but really I'm more of a 'Gunther, the lonely barista' type."

To piggyback on my Robert Redford rant, I also find it amusing that I continuously get students who *want* to be like Jackie O, Michelle Obama, and Ryan Gosling, yet no one ever says they actually *relate* to these stylish, success-ful, seemingly perfect people. I do find that many students say they relate to Liz Lemon (Tina Fey's character) from *30 Rock*, Greg Heffley from *Diary of a Wimpy Kid*, and the title character from *Amélie*.

We relate to people who reveal themselves as genuine, warts and all. Therefore, you should strive to be your most genuine self when telling a tale.

⋛ TELL YOUR STORY ⋛

Fill in the blank. The responses do not have to be tied in with one another, but they can be.

I'M THE TYPE OF GUY/GIRL WHO'LL _____.

I NEVER _____.

BUT I'LL ALWAYS _____.

~~~~~~~~~~~~~~~~~~~~~~~~~~~~~~~~

For me, the answers are:

I'M THE TYPE OF GIRL WHO'LL CHANGE THE CHANNEL IMMEDIATELY TO AVOID WEEPING IF A COMMERCIAL ABOUT ABUSED OR ENDANGERED ANIMALS COMES ON.

I NEVER VISIT DOG SHELTERS (BECAUSE I CANNOT EMOTIONALLY HANDLE IT).

BUT I'LL ALWAYS MAKE A DONATION TO AN ANIMAL CHARITY IF I HAVE ANY MONEY TO SPARE.

⦚ TELL YOUR STORY ⦚

Part two of this exercise is to tell a story that proves one of these statements to be true. Pinpoint the characteristic or quality within yourself that the statement exemplifies and tell a specific story that relates.

~~~~~~~~~~~~~~~~~~~~~~~~

For example, several years ago I watched every season back-to-back of HBO's *The Wire*. In season four, the show dives into the perils of the inner-city Baltimore public school system. At the end of season four, there were some really tough scenes depicting what the future held for these children who had the deck stacked against them. I was so affected by this I was depressed for over a week. I couldn't stop thinking about how messed-up the system was, and how I felt like there was nothing I could do to help. Then one day it occurred to me—I couldn't save all the children of Baltimore, but I could save a dog. I went to a dog rescue site and looked up how much money it would take to get one dog out of a kill shelter. It was within my budget, so I sent in the donation anonymously and saved a dog. And slowly I felt like I could make a small difference in the world.

~~~~~~~~~~~~~~~~~~~~~~~~

A great way to make your story pop and define yourself as a character is the use of nostalgic specifics. I was just working with a student the other day who said she had a lot of childhood crushes. I asked her specifically who she had a crush on, and she said, "Disney princes." I said, "From what movies?" And she said, "The prince from *The Little Mermaid.*" And right there, I had a nostalgic reference for the time period of her youth. That movie came out in 1989, so we can now visualize her swooning over the hot prince from *The Little Mermaid* while wearing a scrunchie in her side ponytail. If she had said, "I had a crush on Shang from *Mulan*" (which came out almost ten years later, in 1998), we would have an image of her swooning over this cartoon heartthrob while wearing platform sneakers and raver pants. Both of these images are much more interesting than simply knowing she had generic childhood crushes.

> *What makes your story a story that only you can tell is how clearly you define yourself as a character.*

Adding nostalgia is also a great way to get a laugh. I tell a story in which I cry in my dorm room while listening to the Indigo Girls. That line always gets a laugh. It's a nostalgic specific that takes us back to a direct time, rather than "I cried and listened to music." And it makes me a specific type of person. Someone who cries while listening to Barbra Streisand's "The Way We Were" is a very different character than someone like me, who would cry while listening to the Indigo Girls' "Power of Two." The student I mentioned above might cry while listening to "Part of Your World." Either way, we know a lot more about the storyteller if we add in these nostalgic specifics.

I teach people of all ages, and often people will worry that an audience won't get their nostalgic references if they didn't grow up in the same era. Well, I can guarantee you that it's highly unlikely that you will ever be telling a story to a group of people who are all the exact same age. Even if your audience is somehow magically all the exact same age, there is no way everyone will remember the exact same things from that era that you do. So all I can say is, commit to your story and vividly sell your memory. I find that if it was memorable enough for you to recall, it's probably something in the zeitgeist that we're all aware of, no matter our age. So whether you got ready for your date by ironing your hair while listening to Joni Mitchell or you got ready for your date by hair-spraying your bangs to an upright position while listening to Whitesnake, most of us will get your nostalgic references. And they make for clearer images than simply "getting ready for a date."

WAYS TO ADD NOSTALGIA TO YOUR STORY

- **What were you wearing?**

Be specific. I just had a good laugh with someone over those early '90s rayon pimp suits. They were usually royal blue or mustard or eggplant, and, in hindsight, were ridiculous. How funny would it be to add into a story taking place in that era "I got ready for the big dance. Put on my best suit ... I was dressed head to toe in purple, and I just knew I wasn't going home alone that night."

Nostalgia stirs up memories we totally forgot about, and it's fun to laugh about our fashion faux pas from the past. Also, what you were wearing shows us what type of person you were at the time. For a story that takes place in the early '80s, you could be wearing a leather jacket with spikes, or boat shoes and a polo shirt. Those conjure up two completely opposite characters. Imagine being able to convey exactly who you were by describing an outfit.

- **What music was playing?**

If you can't remember exactly what was playing, think about what *might* have been playing at the time. A prom story where you slow-dance to the Five Satins' "In the Still of the Night" and a prom story where you slow-dance to Cyndi Lauper's "Time After Time" stir up two very specific and very different places in history for all of us.

- **What type of car were you in?**

Adding nostalgic specifics to a car featured in a story can show us a lot about your personality, or even your economic background. So often storytellers say, "And then we packed into the car." I ask, "What type of car?" Because if you all packed into your stepdad's '82 Toyota Corolla rather than your brand-new BMW convertible, it's a very different image.

- **Who were your idols? Crushes? Role models? Heroes?**

How different is "Growing up I wanted to be cool" versus "Growing up I wanted to be just like Zack Morris on *Saved by the Bell*" versus "Growing up I wanted to be cool, just like Justin Timberlake. I even bleached my curly hair to bring some of that *NSYNC mojo into my own life."

- **What foods did you eat or drink?**

My friend and hilarious storyteller Jenna Brister once told a story in which she came home from school and had her snack, "Gushers, as usual." It made me laugh so hard. Gushers are "naturally flavored" fruit snacks that gush out a sugar/corn syrup/food-colored center when you bite into them. As a mom in today's era of kale chips and seaweed snacks, I cracked up when she took me back to a time when moms could just throw a pack of Gushers at their kids and call it a day.

Drinks can also create clear characters. I tell a story about going out on a date with a meathead who said, "Lemme order you a drink." He then ordered me his favorite drink, Red Bull and vodka. That drink order shows something completely different about that character compared to someone who orders "your finest scotch on the rocks."

> The more specific you are, the more relatable you are.
>
> **—JANEANE GAROFALO,**
> **actress and comedian***

If you are just a generic person from a nonspecific place in time, who dresses nondescriptly, has generic taste in music, fantasizes about no one in particular, and simply eats "food," how can we connect? Well, I was a brooding teenager in the '90s who wore combat boots to school every day and dyed my hair with Manic Panic hair color. I listened to my father's records of the Velvet Underground, the Doors, Janis Joplin, and Jimi Hendrix—I gravitated

---

* I was lucky enough to meet the hilarious Janeane Garofalo, backstage at a storytelling show. This is what she told me that night and it really stuck with me.

toward any rock musician who'd had a tragic demise. I secretly loved Keanu Reeves but thought he was too "mainstream," so I kept it to myself. I was a vegetarian, obviously, and loved that my lack of iron made me even paler, to go along with my brooding rocker-chick look.

So even if that doesn't sound like you, maybe you knew someone like that, or saw someone like that on television. Maybe you even wanted to be someone like that.* However you look at it, those specific nostalgic elements I shared make me much more relatable than simply being "a teenager."

> And there's everybody at my funeral wearing halter tops or chokers or some shit like that.
>
> **—VICKIE (played by Janeane Garofalo),** *Reality Bites*

If you ever look up a musician or band on Wikipedia, often their influences will be listed. For example, if you look up Christina Aguilera, it lists Etta James, Billie Holiday, and Nina Simone, among others. Knowing that

---

* Although I highly doubt it! Believe me, it was a rough time.

about Aguilera, you can see those influences in her music. She's certainly not exactly like the artists who inspired her, but you can see sparks of them in her work. So what about you? Who helped you become who you are?

⋛ TELL YOUR STORY ⋛

• Try listing ten things (people/places/artists/books/ etc.) that inspire you. Is there a through line? Do academic types inspire you? Underdogs? Quirky artists?

• Next, try listing five words that describe you. Are you smart? Altruistic? Clumsy? Often the way we see ourselves is not how others see us.

• Then tack on five things that you want. What you want can be anything from world peace to a really thorough housecleaning service.

• Now look at all you've written down. Your page contains a fascinating fleshed-out character with quirks, dreams, and influences. Look how interesting you are! You are a person anyone would kill to hear a story about.

~~~~~~~~~~~~~~~~~~~~~~~~~~

Q: Okay, I get it, I'm interesting. But what about the other characters in my stories? How do I make them come alive?

A: People waste a lot of time on external characters when telling a story. In Chapter 3, I explained the tactic of creating composite characters. I also said it's okay to cut unnecessary characters out of your tale. What I didn't explain is how to make the remaining characters pop, without taking too much of the emphasis away from you.

Try and find a way to nail down any other characters in a sentence or two. You can always go back to the public-figure method. I have in a past story described a character in a tale by saying, "She looked just like Angelina Jolie and behaved exactly like the insane character she played in *Girl, Interrupted*." And from that single sentence, you get her.

The mistake many folks make is then diving into everything else they can remember about the person. "She was a little older than me, had brown hair, grew up in Wisconsin, drove a Ford Explorer . . ." None of that matters. We already got what we needed to know from the *Girl, Interrupted* sentence. My friend and brilliant storyteller Brian Finkelstein once described a character in a story as a man who "was dipping a chamomile tea bag into an NPR coffee mug." That's it. But it nailed the essence of the character perfectly.

Q: Isn't there an official name for the important characters in a story? I have some vague memory of this from my high school English classes, but then again, I was barely paying attention.

A: Don't worry, English was the only subject I paid attention to in high school. I remember!

• **Flat characters:** Not the main people in the story. Think of them as the characters that would be nominated for best supporting actor/actress at the Oscars. They are essential to the piece, but they're not the ones undergoing major change or development.

• **Round characters:** The best actor/actress category of your story. The round characters most certainly include you, and maybe one other person who develops and experiences change.

For example, in the classic John Hughes movie *Ferris Bueller's Day Off*, Sloane, Ferris's girlfriend, with the fabulous fringed jacket, is a flat character. She is essential to the plot, but nothing really changes in her within the film.

However, in my opinion, *both* Ferris and his best friend, Cameron, are round characters. Ferris is round because the story surrounds him; it's seen through his eyes. He is the lead and also the narrator. But Cameron is actually the character who experiences change.

≷ TELL YOUR STORY ≷

Since you don't have two hours, like a movie does, to tell your story, you have to nail your flat and round characters quickly. Think of a person from your life and try to convey who they are specifically in one or two sentences.

~~~~~~~~~~~~~~~~~~~~~~~~~~~

For example, "My friend Alice is sporty, to say the least. She has a face that one could describe as 'handsome.'"

In that description, we know we are dealing with a character who is athletic, tough, and tomboyish. Also, the beauty of telling a live story is that you are there in person to help flesh yourself out as a character. Anyone I tell this tale to would be able to see that I look fairly feminine and not at all tough, and I don't have a body that screams "athlete" or even "former athlete." So I need only two sentences to set up the fun opposites-attract dynamic of our friendship. Additionally, because the story is about *me*, that's all I need to say about Alice. She is my partner in crime for the tale, but she really doesn't develop or experience change.

⩗ TELL YOUR STORY ⩗

Now take a moment to describe yourself *as you were at the time* of a specific story that happened to you. Since you are a round character, the lead, you can take a little more time with your description, but not too much!

~~~~~~~~~~~~~~~~~~~~~~~~~~~~~~

I'll go back to my night-with-Alice story to show you what I mean: "I was nineteen years old, and I had no money. My bank account had literally zero dollars in it. I was fifteen pounds overweight due to the steady diet I had at the time, which was beer with a side of butter, but I still believed I was one of the hottest chicks around."

And that's all I need to say. My audience knows I was one of those young people who has no idea just how low on the totem pole she really is. I was broke, chubby, and very confident!

> It is my ambition to say in ten sentences what others say in a whole book.
>
> **—FRIEDRICH NIETZSCHE,**
> **philosopher and poet**

CHAPTER 10

ROOTING FOR THE STORYTELLER

We are flawed creatures, all of us.
Some of us think that means we should fix
our flaws. But get rid of my flaws and there
would be no one left.

—SARAH VOWELL,
Take the Cannoli

Think about people/characters/teams you have rooted for in the past. Now think about why. It's likely because you see sincerity in them, vulnerability, or good intentions. Or it could be that he/she/it is a flat-out underdog.

Now, think about people/characters/teams you have turned away from. Maybe you initially were rooting for them but now, not so much. Maybe there is even a television show you were watching and then suddenly stopped. Sure, maybe you stopped watching because you no longer had the time, or your favorite actor/actress left the show. But it's more probable that you stopped because you were no longer rooting for the character you were rooting for in the first place.

You may have even seen something like this play out in person. If you have access to live shows in your area, maybe you've watched a stand-up comedian lose or alienate the crowd right from the top and never get them back. Maybe you've seen an episode of the aforementioned *Shark Tank* where an entrepreneur lost the interest of the "Sharks" and just couldn't get it back. Maybe you've watched a guest on a talk show bomb an interview for whatever reason.

You may have seen something like this happen at a religious service, when a priest/rabbi/etc. loses the crowd. For example, I was once at a bar mitzvah where the rabbi spoke graphically for over twenty minutes about circumcision. Not only did it cross the line into being inappropriate, it made a lot of people uncomfortable and felt like

IT'S EASY to GET US on YOUR SIDE, BUT IT'S HARD to GET US BACK ONCE YOU'VE LOST US it went on forever. It's all I remember about that service, actually, despite spending hours there.

The same goes for TV, or books, or films. Once you are no longer cheering for anyone, you are out. Some shows are tricky; they switch around the character we are rooting for. For example, *Breaking Bad* had us either rooting for Walt, Jesse, or both, but always for someone. Other shows switch around who the home team is (there was a major shake-up between seasons three and four of *Friday Night Lights*) or who the business partners are (*Mad Men* has swapped out and added partners, and changed offices many times) so we can continue to root for someone. It's harder for us to root for the football team that never loses or the consistently successful ad agency, so these shows don't let their characters get too comfortable in certain team formations or hierarchies.

> *We root for underdogs, plain and simple.*
> *Be an underdog in your story.*

What makes you an underdog? What have you struggled with in the past or even on a daily basis? What are you bad at? Sports? Dating? Keeping a job?

{ *Don't force shortcomings that
are insincere.* }

I am more than a little sick of stunningly beautiful celebrities who have been famous since age twelve discussing in interviews how they were ugly ducklings when they were younger. I always think, "When was this person's awkward stage? Because I've seen her grow up on my TV for the past twenty years and she's never been anything but drop-dead gorgeous." I am also a little sick of the cool kids calling themselves nerds. I always think about how you never see people like Stephen Hawking, Jane Goodall, or Richard Dawkins referring to themselves as "like a total nerd."

So why would we root for *you*? Are you bad with guys/girls? Were you overweight in high school and no one would know that by looking at you now? If you're seemingly together and attractive, this could be a disadvantage for you when telling a tale. Sometimes we are quicker to root for someone who is more of a Seymour than an Audrey.*

---

* What, you didn't get my *Little Shop of Horrors* reference? You can take the girl out of the theater major, but . . . you know how the saying goes.

Just like I said in the Chapter 9, you either have to combat or work with what we're already thinking about you. Often, in stories, I acknowledge my size (I'm five foot ten). While to some people in the audience, my height comes off as intimidating (something I don't want to be), to others it may seem enviable. I try to find ways to combat that—when I approach a microphone and have to adjust it up, I often say something like, "Sorry, give me a second here—the performer before me wasn't a hulking woman like myself, so I've got to raise this up." Or I'll make a joke about my outfit: "Does this look okay? It's supposed to be a dress for every other woman, but for me, it's a crop top." These small and silly statements instantly make me an underdog, as the audience then sees my struggle with being tall, rather than seeing my height as something to be envious or scared of.

Conveniently, I recently received a lovely e-mail from a former student, Drew Cohn, on this exact topic. This guy is good-looking, with a great head of hair and a likable personality. So how does he convey himself as an underdog without being insincere? Well, he told me in his e-mail that he recently went on an all-male athletic retreat through his church, and at the end anyone who wanted to speak in front of the group had the opportunity to.

"I watched several people speak, and as I formulated my story, I paid attention to what was interesting and effective or not," he wrote. "I remembered what you said as to why we root for someone and what makes us likable or unlikable. One guy went up there and bragged, and he was immediately unlikable. As I'm choosing what to say in my head, my heart rate is up and I'm nervous . . . I start with 'There are a lot of tough guys in here: mentally, physically, and emotionally. I wasn't the most popular guy in my high school, so I was battling a lot of thinking habits and emotions this weekend.' Immediately, they were hooked because I acknowledged and embraced the tough guys in the room and also showed that I had flaws and wasn't perfect. I think every guy in there was already relating."

> I'm interested in flawed protagonists. I was raised on them.
> **—LAURA DERN, actress**

⋛ TELL YOUR STORY ⋚

Think of a time when you won something you didn't expect to win *or* a time when you lost something you were expecting to win but still took something positive from that experience. Recall that story and think of key points that would make others root for you.

~~~~~~~~~~~~~~~~~~~~~~~~~

I use the term "win" loosely. A win doesn't have to mean winning the game, the grand prize, or homecoming king (although it can mean those things). A win can be getting the guy/girl, the part, or the job, or getting into a college, grad school, etc.

NOTABLE UNDERDOGS

• Rudy from the film *Rudy*: a football player who has always been told he is too small to play football

• The Boston Red Sox: a baseball team that allegedly fell victim to "The Curse of the Bambino," which some believe caused the eighty-six-year gap between World Series wins

• J. K. Rowling: the best-selling author, who was on Britain's equivalent of welfare before publishing the Harry Potter books

- Tina Fey: a huge television and movie star and writer, who rose from being behind the scenes as a writer for *Saturday Night Live* to being one of its biggest on-camera stars
- Susan Boyle: a pudgy, awkward woman in her forties who claimed she had never been kissed, who went on *Britain's Got Talent* and wowed the judges with her powerful singing voice, going on to become a household name in music
- Martin Luther King Jr.: I think we all know who MLK is, right?
- Daniel LaRusso (played by Ralph Macchio) in *The Karate Kid*: a lanky new kid in town who learns to master the art of karate in order to defeat his bullies

> Conceal a flaw, and the world
> will imagine the worst.
> **—MARCUS VALERIUS
> MARTIALIS, Roman poet**

If you present yourself as flawless, we won't be on board with you at the top of your piece, and there is often no turning back. On the flip side, it's very easy to get us on board with you from the start. I was just teaching a class where a student was telling a story about a disastrous play in college and I asked her which college it was. She responded, "Yale, but I think I want to leave that out." Her instincts were correct. By simply recounting the tale as a college adventure, everyone can easily root for her, as she was a clear underdog in her story about trying to get into the school play. But if she were to identify the college as Yale, she'd no longer seem like an underdog to the audience. Instead, she'd be a student at one of the best colleges in the country with one of the top theater schools in the country.*

Simple adjustments can get us on board with you much quicker. So don't start stories with details that may come off as bragging.

SMALL THINGS THAT CAN TURN A CROWD AGAINST YOU

• Complaining about an opportunity most people would kill for, e.g., talking about how terrible the food was on the set of the movie you booked a part in
• Name-dropping
• Identifying an elite club/university/group you are involved in by name

---

* Believe me, I know. Have I mentioned I was a theater major?

- Bragging about your sexual prowess
- Having bad intentions
- Being a bully
- Being too cool to be affected by your story, e.g., "Then she dumped me, and I was like, 'Whatever, bitch. See ya later!'" We'll be more likely to root for someone who says, "Then she dumped me, and what I said was, 'Whatever,' but what I meant was, 'Okay, I am positive I will be dying alone now.'"

In order to really connect with your audience, you have to put your flaws out there and incorporate them into your piece.

⋛ TELL YOUR STORY ⋛

Fill in the blank.

_____ IS MY BIGGEST STRENGTH.

_____ IS MY BIGGEST FLAW.

I WISH I COULD BE MORE LIKE ____.

BUT INSTEAD I AM MORE LIKE ____.

DON'T ACT LIKE
YOU'RE TOO COOL
TO CARE.

BE **FRAGILE!**

BE BROKEN!
BE FLAWED!

Now try to isolate a story from your life where your biggest flaw is apparent. Start that story with the phrase *I am a very* _____ *person*. If you're ignorant/ competitive/ overly optimistic/jaded/whatever it may be, I am sure you can think of a specific instance where that played out.

~~~~~~~~~~~~~~~~~~~~~~~~~~~~~~~~~

For example, I am a very open person. I put it all out there and often people respond very well to it, but sometimes I say too much. One night I was at a bar in New York City and really hitting it off with a very cool-looking and professionally put-together woman. I never look professional; in fact, I usually fight my desire to dress like Stevie Nicks circa 1975 , which only is appropriate in very specific settings. It was one of those fun nights out with friends, where everyone is socializing with everyone in the establishment. The woman started showing me pictures on her phone of her adorable niece. I, at the time, had no children and no nieces or nephews, but I felt I had to show her something in return. I looked at the most recent photo I had on my phone; it was a photo of dog poop on the street that was shaped exactly like a penis. Without thinking, I pulled out the picture and said, "Your niece is adorable, but get this. On my way here, I saw this—a poop shaped just like a dick! Can you believe it?"

The woman's facial expression changed immediately, and I knew she was horrified. She was speechless as she shook her head and walked away from me. Then she gathered her things and left the bar. All because of my poop picture. At least I got a story out of it!

Q: What about rooting against someone else in my story? Does that help an audience root more for me?

A: Yes! We will root for you more if you have a clear nemesis. A nemesis can be someone, but it can also be *something* working against you, such as being cursed with it always raining on your birthday. Or some hex over your wedding day, which seems to be doing everything possible to ruin it. A nemesis can be a substance, like drugs or alcohol, or something you are allergic to but still love. A nemesis can also be an animal or pet, or a machine, like your car or computer. It can be something broad, such as technology or school, or superspecific, like a certain song or a town you frequently visit.

In stand-up comedy, it is sometimes an advantage to have a cocky persona (like Daniel Tosh, Dane Cook, or Anthony Jeselnik, to name a few); in storytelling, the opposite is true. The more vulnerable and flawed you are, the higher you will soar. Doesn't that sound a lot easier than trying to act like you have it all?

FAMOUS NEMESES

- Lex Luthor to Superman
- Snakes to Indiana Jones
- Newman to Jerry on *Seinfeld*
- New York City to George Kellerman in *The Out of Towners*
- Heroin to William S. Burroughs in the book *Junkie*
- Lucy to Charlie Brown

} *Don't be afraid to let your shortcomings shine.* {

≳ TELL YOUR STORY ≲

Name ten public figures who were honest about a less-than-perfect quality and were rewarded for it.

~~~~~~~~~~~~~~~~~~~~~~

Really think about how much we celebrate imperfect people. Would you like Oprah Winfrey more or less if all you knew about her was she was a billionaire who had one of the most successful talk shows ever? If Bill Clinton had hidden the fact that he was raised by an alcoholic, abusive stepfather, would you have been as inspired by his rise to success?

Now that you're on your way to becoming a vulnerable, flawed storyteller that your audience will want to root for, it's time to start building that portfolio of stories. I have an exercise that will push you to tell a story about something you never expected to talk about.

⋛ TELL YOUR STORY ⋚

I call this "The Asshole Exercise." Think of a time in your life when you behaved less than perfectly, perhaps a time where you didn't take the high road. Write down some notes on why an audience/listener may still root for you. Make us believe you aren't an asshole even though you may have done the so-called "wrong thing."

— DON'T PORTRAY — YOURSELF AS PERFECT. AS MUCH AS WE ROOT FOR THE UNDERDOG, WE ALSO ROOT FOR A PERFECT PERSON TO BE TORN DOWN

IF YOUR INTENTIONS are GOOD, EVEN if YOU DIDN'T DO the "RIGHT THING," WE'LL STILL BE on BOARD

CHAPTER 11

THE FULL CIRCLE

You know, I'll probably die just a few miles
from where I drew my first breath.

**—LYNDON BAINES JOHNSON,
36th president of the United States**

Q: I love when I watch a movie or hear a story or read a book that ends exactly as it begins. How can I do that in my own stories?

A: Often, when students ask me how to end their stories, I tell them to go back and look at their very first sentence. Sometimes the end is the same as the beginning. So if you were to start a thesis-based story with a statement like "I will do anything to avoid conflict," your ending might reflect the very same statement. You might want to add a slight adjustment to it, such as "So needless to say, after hiding in the closet twice, wearing a disguise in public, and avoiding the entire state of Kentucky, yes, I *will* do anything to avoid conflict." It's a simple little way to bring your story full circle, and your audience will love it. It will make them feel like they're in on a private joke with you.

You may have heard this technique referred to as "the callback" (different from the acting term of "callback," when an actor gets to come back in to audition for a second time because they did so well at the first audition). A callback in storytelling simply refers toward the end of the story to something said at the beginning of the story, but in a different context. It's a technique you often see in comedy too. If done well, it's really rewarding for the audience, as it creates the feeling of us all being in this together. A good example of this is in Aziz Ansari's comedy special *Dangerously Delicious*, where he discusses some of his dating problems and ends many different jokes with some variation of "I'll go talk to my friend Brian—he's always nice to me." He presents multiple dating dilemmas and repeatedly comes back to his friend Brian, who is nice to him, each time to greater and greater applause and laughter. Worth checking out!

The **full-circle story** ends exactly where it begins, yet something has always changed.

There are many famous stories that come full circle. I know I've mentioned *The Wizard of Oz* before, but I am assuming most of you will have seen it and understand the references. Also, it's no coincidence it's such a classic, as it is a fantastic example of storytelling. When Dorothy returns back to her home in Kansas at the end, and the film goes back to black and white, sure, all is exactly as the film began. But something has changed. Our main character has grown from her experiences and now goes back to her original life with a new perspective. It's a fantastic and organic full circle.

> *Full circles in your story can be magical, but don't force a connection that isn't there. That will turn your audience against you.*

EXAMPLES OF FORCED FULL CIRCLES

· **Looking up what happened to the other party in your story on social media/the Internet instead of running into them in person.**

I have never been riveted by someone recounting a recent Google search. And in all my years of teaching and performing, I have heard more live storytelling than almost anyone. I have only heard two social media–based stories ever that I have been really captivated by—one about a Facebook misunderstanding and one about a Twitter embarrassment. The best stories tend to happen face-to-face. So when life throws a moment at you like being a hot mess in front of the ex you haven't seen in twelve years (more details on this embarrassing moment later), it's much more suited for the stage than a story that ends "And I looked him up on Facebook, and guess what— still cute!" If you haven't had an in-person encounter with the other character in your tale since it happened, there is no need to force a full circle.*

• **Purposefully returning to the setting of your story to give it an ending.**

Of course, there are exceptions to this, especially in stories more journalistic in nature. Often the subject in a jour- nalistic story will return back to the scene of the crime, etc. for more facts on the situation. But when it comes to

---

* Of course if you look a person up and what you discover is shocking and story worthy—such as your shy science teacher now working as a Neil Diamond impersonator in Vegas—then maybe it could work. I just hear a lot of stories ending with "Her Facebook status says 'married' now," and I would prefer a story of running into the ex and her new husband.

telling stories, I prefer when life events naturally take you back to your original haunts. I find it really exciting when events such as a wedding or reunion force us to return to places, relationships, or social circles we never expected we'd be revisiting.

- **Creating a manufactured moment instead of having a moment recur naturally in your life.**

Once when I was in college in Ithaca, NY, I had a spooky experience where both my friend Seth and I saw the identical image of a boy in a red sweatshirt run past the top of a flight of stairs in Seth's house at the exact same time. Although neither of us are all that into the supernatural, it was a strange experience because of the simultaneous sighting. It's really Seth's story to tell in full, but the gist of it is, there were many strange occurrences in his house that happened after that sighting, including other sightings by other roommates of the exact same boy.

Eight years passed, and I questioned many times whether or not that really happened; I just couldn't believe I saw a ghost. Until one day my now husband and I went back to Ithaca to look at wedding venues. We chose to get married there because we both had ties to the area (some of his relatives had lived there). My husband had told me that he wanted to visit his grandmother's grave during our trip, and if we also had time, he'd like to see the house where I saw the ghost. He had heard the story so many times, and he wanted to put an image to it.

When we briefly swung by that creepy house, my husband begged me to retell him the full story of the boy in the red sweatshirt. After I told him, he said stunned, "Wait, that house? Right there? The one next to that plot of land? Because at the other end of that plot of land is a small old graveyard where my grandmother is buried. So, I'm pretty sure you saw a ghost."

Now, if I had specifically taken a trip to Ithaca to find an ending to my ghost story, it wouldn't have been organic. But life circumstances took me back to Ithaca years later and while I was there I accidentally got closure I didn't plan on.

> *Dramatic life events make the best stories when they unfold coincidentally. When a story is too perfect, it can come off as concocted.*

So much of our life comes full circle without us even realizing it. We find ourselves back at significant places, reconnecting with old friends, recycling lovers, repeating the same patterns, yet we have grown since the last time we were in this position.

⋛ TELL YOUR STORY ⋛

Recall a time your life came full circle. Think about how you ended up exactly where you began, and what happened and changed in between. If you ended up growing and changing (just like Dorothy), then it's worth exploring as one of your go-to stories.

~~~~~~~~~~~~~~~~~~~~~~~~~

I have had many full circles occur in my life. In one of them, I dated someone when I was right out of college living in New York City. It was my first adult relationship, but I was far from an adult, and so was he. We basically danced, drank, laughed, and hooked up for about eight months. I was just figuring out what I wanted to do with my life, and so was he. At the time of our breakup, I was frequently hungover, often stoned, and completely irresponsible. Since our breakup, he's gone on to succeed in his field of business, purchased a home, and gotten married. I have gotten married, had a baby, and succeeded in my field as well. In the year after my son was born, I went away on my own for a weekend only one time, to the wedding of my college roommate. At the wedding, as a new mom needing a little break, I partied like I was still in college. The next day

I was at the airport, reeking of pot, still a little drunk from the night before, and a total hot mess.*

Waiting at the terminal, I ran into my ex, the first guy I'd dated out of college. When he approached me, all I could think was, "Oh my God. I'm exactly where he left me twelve years ago, hungover and reeking of marijuana." During the entire conversation, I had to fight the urge to say, "I have a savings account and health insurance and a dog. I swear I've grown up!" But instead, this guy caught me on the *one* "morning after" partying in this manner that I'd had in more than two years. I found myself in the exact state of mind I had been in twelve years ago, with the exact same person, yet so much had changed since that time.

> A good [story] would take me out of myself and then stuff me back in, out-sized, now, and uneasy with the fit.
> —DAVID SEDARIS, *Children Playing Before a Statue of Hercules*

---

* Actually, I'd take the "hot" out of the "hot mess." Really I was just a mess.

EXAMPLES OF GOOD FULL CIRCLES

- The character arc of Nate Fisher (Peter Krause) on *Six Feet Under*
- The arc of Princess Ann (Audrey Hepburn) in *Roman Holiday*
- The film version of *The Outsiders*
- The arc of Frank Farmer (Kevin Costner) in *The Bodyguard**
- The song "Cat's in the Cradle" by Harry Chapin
- David Sedaris's essay "Repeat After Me"
- The Coen brothers' film *Inside Llewyn Davis*
- The Simon & Garfunkel song "Overs"
- *Animal Farm* by George Orwell
- *If You Give a Mouse a Cookie* by Laura Numeroff
- The film *Coming to America*

I assure you, these full-circle moments are frequent in life. But the mistake many storytellers make, is to manufacture the full circle to give their story an ending. Forced full circles are disrespectful to your audience, who has invested time in your story.

---

* Don't hate on me for citing *The Bodyguard* as a good reference point. I love that movie unironically.

Q: So how do I recognize the full circles within my own life? I'm not a professional storyteller; I may have missed some that have already happened.

A: Start recognizing patterns in your own life; therein lies the full circle.

1. Recall places you have returned, and think about why. Have you gone back to your college town? Your hometown? The company where you got your first job? A city you keep vacationing in?

2. When have you had the thought "Why does this keep happening to me?" For example, in middle school I had a humiliating experience in the school cafeteria. Then in college, once I was out of my awkward phase and coming into my own, I had an even more humiliating experience also in a cafeteria. Although I had changed, the location of my humiliation, even though it was hundreds of miles from the first time, was still a cafeteria.

3. What types of people do you keep attracting? The crazy friend? The embarrassing boyfriend?

4. What types of jobs do you keep getting? Maybe the job changes, but other things remain consistent, such as awful coworkers, or office romances you regret.

5. What about family stuff? What role do you repeatedly take in your family: the kid sister, the "bad cop" parent, the sulking teenager?

6. Have you ever had the thought "Oh no, I've turned into my mother/my father/my elementary school teacher/my grandparent"? There is also a full-circle story there.

Remember, don't spell it out for us by saying, "It all came full circle when . . ." Let the full circle be a fun moment that ties your story together. Sometimes simply repeating or paraphrasing the beginning of your story does the trick.

And now, my chapter on the full circle has come full circle.

CHAPTER 12

SOMEONE ELSE'S STORY

I really haven't had that exciting
of a life . . . I'd rather tell a story
about somebody else.

—KURT COBAIN, musician

———————————————

Many of my students want to tell stories they were not
present for, such as the story of how their parents met. I
say, let your parents tell that story. Sure, you can incorporate bits of your parents' tale to inform your own story,
as in "My parents met in college at age nineteen, so when
my twentieth birthday rolled around and I still hadn't
had my first kiss, I knew it wasn't going to be that easy for
me." But most people would rather hear how *you* met *your*

significant other.* The emotion that tale will stir up for you will drive that story to be an instant success.

Think about it socially—wouldn't you rather hear a close friend recount a recent dating disaster that happened to him/her, rather than hear a close friend recount his/her brother's recent dating debacle? We're not playing telephone here; we're storytelling!

Again, I keep coming back to telling stories with a clear conscience. You wouldn't want someone else publicly telling the story of your most embarrassing moment, would you?

> Every time you consider telling someone else's tale, ask yourself these two questions:
>
> **1.** Is there a personal story from my own life that will show the same thing?
> **2.** Would I be comfortable with someone else telling this story about me if I were not there to tell it?

---

* This is my personal opinion, but I see audiences react stronger to this method almost every time.

Of course, as I have said many times, there are exceptions to everything. But I truly believe in storytelling as a way to connect with others. And remember, telling stories exclusively about other people's lives can be seen as gossip.

I do think that great stories can be made from sharing experiences of events you were present for but not the star, such as a crazy thing you witnessed. However, this does come with its challenges. To tell that kind of story, you must insert yourself into the story often, not just recount what you saw.

Q: But Margot, if I am merely witnessing something, how can I insert myself into the story? It's not like it happened to me.

A: The inner monologue! Inner monologue shows the audience what you were thinking at the time of an event. It can turn a two-minute story into a ten-minute story. You can also use this technique when you are the star, by the way.

To show you how to use inner monologue to your advantage, here's an example of a story about something I witnessed:

"As my date and I sat awkwardly across from each other trying to figure out what to order, a woman two tables down stood up and began to scream, 'Everyone stop eating right now! There is blood in my chicken! I didn't want to have to do this, but you wouldn't take it off the bill!' And as she slowly walked backward out the door, with each step she took she screamed, 'There. Is. Blood. In. My. Chicken!' Then she exited. I was thrilled. This was pretty much the most exciting thing that could happen on a first date—drama unfolding right before our eyes. I wanted to stand up and applaud her performance. Her exit had as much panache as Richard Nixon boarding that helicopter as he waved a victory sign in the air. Now my date and I would have something to instantly bond over. Shared drama, a private joke. Perfect! But when I managed to pry my eyes off the door, I looked across the table to find my date's head buried in his menu. Finally, he looked up. 'I'm so sorry, Margot,' he said. 'Sorry for what?' I said. 'That's like the best thing that could have happened! It was hilarious! You didn't watch that?' 'No,' he said, 'I avert my eyes when things like that happen.' We were ten minutes into the date, and I already knew we weren't a match. Anyone who didn't see real-life drama as a free show we are privileged to watch was not the guy for me. Now I had to sit through an awkward dinner with someone I was rapidly starting to dislike."

So now, instead of this being a story about "the crazy chicken lady," it becomes a very relatable story about

YOU MAY NOT HAVE ACTIVELY BEEN A PART OF AN EVENT YOU'VE SEEN, BUT INNER MONOLOGUE CAN MAKE IT *YOUR* STORY knowing instantly that someone just isn't right for you. The rest of that story focuses on my date and me, but I continue to reference the chicken lady throughout.

WAYS TO TRIGGER INNER MONOLOGUE WHEN TELLING SOMEONE ELSE'S STORY

• Did you fantasize about how you would handle the situation you witnessed?

• How did you justify the situation you saw before you? (For example, "When the man dressed as a pirate walked into the hotel, I thought, 'It must be Halloween.' Then I remembered I had just celebrated Thanksgiving and I thought, 'It's definitely not Halloween.'"

• What was your opinion on what was happening?

• Did you enjoy what happened before you or did have a negative reaction to what you saw?

• Did you take sides?

• Did you imagine an explanation so the events would make sense?

A TO Z VERSUS A TO B

A-to-Z thoughts are all the crazy things we think but never dare to say out loud. And when inner-monologue-ing, you have to go from A to Z; you can't just go from A to B. On my chicken-lady date, the A-to-B inner monologue would be: "This date isn't going well. He seems scared of real-life drama. We are definitely not a match." But that only scratches the surface.

Here's the A-to-Z version of that same train of thought:

"Oh my God! He didn't think that bloody chicken drama was hilarious. We're not going to connect on anything. Should I leave right now? Maybe I can pretend my phone is on silent and step out to take an 'emergency phone call' and then tell him my grandmother is in the hospital and I have to go. He'll never find out my grandmother died in 1992, right? That was before Google. But if I slip out, I'm not giving him a chance. My friend Jessica, who set us up, said we'd be a match. Why did she think that? I'm kind of insulted. Note to self: Call Jessica when this date is over. Okay, he's smiling at me. I should smile back. I should give him a try. Otherwise, I could die an old spinster."

When trying to convey A-to-Z thoughts, try to remember the worst or best possible scenario your mind came up with. So if you were recounting waiting for a job interview

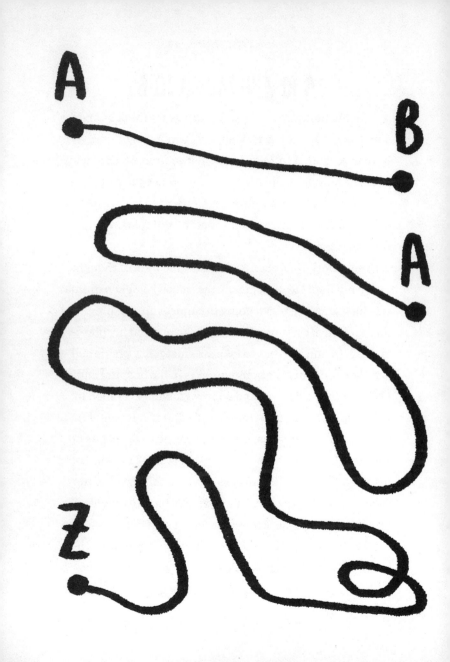

while hearing the candidate before stay in the interview room extralong and repeatedly make the interviewer laugh, the A-to-Z *best* possible scenario might be "That interviewer seems really jovial. I'm funny too. I can win him over and nail this. Then I'll have health insurance and I can go to the dentist and have really clean teeth. I'll get massages when my back hurts and see a podiatrist just because I can. Put me in, coach! Mama needs a checkup!"

The A-to-Z *worst* possible scenario might be: "Wow, she's been in there thirty minutes. What is this, her half-hour Comedy Central stand-up special? I'm not funny. I didn't realize you had to have gone to clown college to get a job doing data entry. Great. Now, I'll still be unemployed. I'll never have health insurance. And forget about dental. My teeth will rot out of my mouth, and I'll look like a hill-billy. No one will hire me if I look like a hillbilly. Oh, she's killing it again. This time she's gotten a belly laugh. I'm doomed. Crest Whitestrips, here I come."

> But inside, I'm going, "Oh my God, is my zipper up? Do I have a booger in my nose?" That's my inner monologue.
>
> **—LEAH REMINI, actress**

⋛ TELL YOUR STORY ⋛

Think of a time you witnessed a seemingly perfect person get torn down. We see this all the time in the media (e.g., Britney Spears, Tiger Woods, John Edwards), but try and recount a situation from your own life when you witnessed the perfect outer layers begin to get stripped from a person you knew. Tell their story from your perspective, inserting your inner monologue, reactions, theory of what happened, etc.

~~~~~~~~~~~~~~~~~~~~~~~~

A good example of a story about someone else was told by one of my very first students, Nathaniel Cocca-Bates. He recounted a childhood D.A.R.E. (Drug Abuse Resistance Education) teacher he idolized. He built up this teacher, Chuck, as his hero—not only was he the father of a big local football star, but he was a Vietnam veteran with a Purple Heart. Nathaniel spoke of how much it meant to him the day Chuck brought that medal to class, and what it felt like to touch it. He spoke of how he wrote the best personal essay opposing drugs and how he felt so strongly about it that he cried when he read it aloud. He wanted to be just like his cool teacher Chuck.

Years later, when Nathaniel was a teenager, Chuck was exposed by an angry ex-wife as being a total fraud. (He had

TELLING A TALE ABOUT SOMEONE ELSE ISN'T AN EXCUSE TO SPREAD GOSSIP. IT'S A CHANCE TO SHARE YOUR PERSPECTIVE ON A MEMORABLE SITUATION posed his son for pictures in a football jersey—his son was never on a team. He had bought the Purple Heart at an estate sale.) My student Nathaniel's world came crashing down on him. D.A.R.E. was bullshit, he thought, and so was Chuck. He told the story of Chuck's fall from grace intertwined with his own personal journey with such emotion I still remember it today.

> If you don't tell your story, someone else will.
>
> **—UNKNOWN**

CHAPTER 13

THE UNEXPECTED

The marvels of daily life are exciting;
no movie director can arrange the
unexpected that you find in the street.

**—ROBERT DOISNEAU,
photographer**

If we know exactly where your story is headed, then why should we listen? Great stories throw us for a loop and take us somewhere we never anticipated. Adding an element of the unexpected into your tale can really make it soar.

Think about some examples of times you were shocked by an unexpected twist in film, literature, or television.

Sure, films like *The Usual Suspects*, *The Sixth Sense*, and *Citizen Kane* are often cited as having brilliantly unexpected twists. But what examples come to mind of unexpected twists from your own life?

Here's a way to help dig out some gems that are hiding in the back of your brain.

⋛ TELL YOUR STORY ⋚

Think of a day from your life that you expected to be one of the best that turned out to be one of the worst. Perhaps a vacation gone awry? Or starting your dream job that turned out to be more of a nightmare? Or think of a day from your life that you expected to be one of the worst days ever that actually turned out to be great. Perhaps a funeral that ended up bringing long-lost relatives? Or a day you were so sad after a breakup that you end up adopting the best dog ever to help you through your struggle? Life is filled with unexpected twists!

~~~~~~~~~~~~~~~~~~~~~~~~~~~~~~~~~~~

I have said this before, but I really mean it: trust the intelligence of your listeners. Say you're telling a story to your friends. Well, you're probably friends with these people because you have a lot in common. You aren't friends with

DON'T LET YOUR AUDIENCE GET TEN STEPS AHEAD OF YOU

dummies, so you can expect your friends to put two and two together when you spill your guts to them. If you're telling a story in the workplace, perhaps at a company-wide presentation, remember that your coworkers all got hired because of shared characteristics and skill levels. They're no dopes—they can figure out where your story is headed. So don't tell a story that everyone predicts the ending of in the first minute.

I think of this often when I read bedtime stories to my toddler son. Of course I know where the story is going, because these books are geared for the under-three crowd, and I am in my thirties. But my son remains shocked every time that the duck finds its way back home! So remember who your audience is. And play to that audience.

I had a very naturally gifted storyteller in one of the early classes I taught in New York City, a playwright named Joel Jones, who now teaches storytelling himself in Virginia. What I loved about Joel, is you never knew what direction his story was taking, and he wasn't afraid to go dark. He wasn't seeking audience approval; he was sharing his truth.

The story he ended up telling in the class performance was incredibly unexpected. It was about how he's a "boyfriend guy," a person immediately perceived as boyfriend material. He was sick of this reputation, and so many years ago, before going out to a local bar, his friend mentioned that a woman named "Karen" would be there who "would like you to have a drink with her." His friend went on to say that the woman "was tired of dating and wants to settle down." Joel knew this woman and didn't care for her. He didn't want to have to spend his whole night talking with someone he didn't care for. So that night, he went to the local bar and instead of being the "boyfriend guy," he blew her off. She sat inside, and Joel sat outside. And when he went in to use the bathroom, she flipped her hair at him flirtatiously, yet Joel kept walking. After that, the woman stormed out.

"And when she got home," Joel said. "We found out later because this is a small town—when Karen got home, she killed herself."

Up until this point in the story, Joel was getting many laughs about his one night out attempting to be the cool single guy. It seemed to be a lighthearted, casual story about the night he decided to change his dating habits and others' expectations of him. But the story wasn't about that at all. It took a dark, unexpected turn and then went to an even more expected place after that. You might think the story would now be about how much he regretted blowing her off, how he felt like he caused a tragic suicide, how he wished he had just been a nice guy like he usually was.

But instead, Joel said, "Now obviously it wasn't *about me* or *because of me*. Obviously, we barely knew each other. I was just the arbitrary name written in the blank. The pivot where the apparatus of her pain swung around. But I *was* the arbitrary name, I *was* the pivot, and that's strange."*

And then he wrapped it all up with a further element of the unexpected. Instead of saying something generic like "I hope she's at peace now," he said, "I don't think I could have been nicer at the time . . . I needed to rebel. Maybe that's what she was doing too. Mostly I feel, despite my rebellion, that it would be wrong to forget her, and wrong to pretend I was important, and in that way I end up the mere passive road for her dramatic journey, the platform for her higher-stakes drama, as if I ended up the 'boyfriend guy' after all."

~~~~~~~~~~~~~~~~~~~~~~~~~~~

The unexpected is similar to "the reversal," a term you may be familiar with if you've ever done fiction or screenplay writing. Usually, in a reversal, a character's status changes. It's the moment in a J. Lo movie when her character decides, "Enough is enough! I am not going to

---

* This is also a great example of how perspective helps a story. Imagine if he had told this story weeks, instead of years, after it happened! He never would have had that hindsight.

be pushed around by my controlling husband anymore. I'm going to learn to kickbox, get out of this town, and get a quiet new life on a lake renting out kayaks." A reversal has to make sense with the rest of the plot, however. J. Lo can't suddenly be able to fly fighter jets if nothing leading up to this moment has shown her already knowing how to fly planes or learning how to fly planes.

The same goes for the unexpected in your story. We need to understand the facts of the situation first so the unexpected twist makes sense. In the above story by Joel Jones, he specified exactly why he blew off "Karen," and how he's normally not like that. That detail makes us really feel how shocked Joel must have been to discover that Karen killed herself the one time he ignored someone who liked him.

> A truly stable system expects the unexpected, is prepared to be disrupted, waits to be transformed.
>
> **—TOM ROBBINS,**
> *Even Cowgirls Get the Blues*

The downside of adding an element of the unexpected is that sometimes an unexpected twist needs longer to develop than the short time you have to tell a story. Films, television shows, and books, all have the freedom to really build trust in a character, so that when that character takes an unexpected turn, the audience is really shocked. In live storytelling, time is limited.

I recently had a student who tried to tell the story of her involvement in a very widely known public hoax within the ten minutes of stage time she was allotted. Think along the lines of Orson Welles's radio adaptation of *The War of the Worlds*, Howard Hughes's fake autobiography, the "Paul McCartney is dead" hoax, and the Hitler Diaries. The story was fascinating. However, in order to understand the unexpected twist of everything being a hoax, the audience first needed to understand what they were faking and what was at stake to keep this facade up. Then, we needed to fully understand the storyteller's perspective on everything happening. We were ten minutes into the story before the student even got to the part about everything being a lie and the unraveling that occurred when they were all found out.

Even my recounting of her recounting is hard to follow. So the downside of twists is that often you need more time than a five- to ten-minute story to lay all the groundwork to make an unexpected element really soar. In fact, I've read a book about the Howard Hughes autobiography hoax (aptly titled *The Hoax*, by Clifford Irving), and it was over three hundred pages long!

Your story needs to make sense to us. It needs to be in layman's terms. So if you've tried recounting an unexpected tale to friends and you've found yourself repeatedly saying, "No, wait, you don't understand," then maybe this tale is best fully developed into a longer-format work, such as a one-person show, screenplay, television series, or book.

We also need to believe it if you got duped, shafted, or conned. Again, you don't want your audience to be ten steps ahead of you thinking, "Of course this guy is going to rob you. Why are you getting in his car?" You don't want to watch a live storytelling performance the same way you watch a horror movie. Your audience shouldn't be screaming out loud, "Do not go into the woods alone! There are obviously zombies in there! Your boyfriend just got eaten alive! Why are you running toward the exact place he just got devoured?!"

BE AUTHENTIC

Don't be fake; we'll see right through that. I tell a story about the first time I discovered the Internet . . . in the late '90s, way after I should have heard of it. I understand this is a tough pill for most audiences to swallow, and it runs the risk of me sounding dumb. It's hard to believe, but it's true, and it's also what's unexpected about this story. Everything that happens after this relies on the audience believing this unexpected thing about me, and how the day unravels because I don't understand what the Internet is. I justify it by having an entire college classroom berate me saying things like "What the hell are you talking about? You've never used the Internet? What have you been doing the past few years?" And my response? I say, "What have I been doing the past few years? I don't know. Dancing in a field with a scarf?"

And with that, something that may seem inauthentic becomes authentic. The audience understands that I was a weirdo teenager who didn't notice things normal kids were noticing. As long as you are being truthful, just take a quick moment to justify yourself, and then go on with your story. Are there going to be one or two audience members who don't believe me? Sure. Does it matter? No.

⋛ TELL YOUR STORY ⋛

Recall a time you got proven wrong. Try and stir up a
memory of something/someone you thought would be
a certain way and was the complete opposite. Maybe
you were completely thrown off by the kindness of an
unlikely person? Or a time you were certain something
happened one way but when you researched it you discovered you were completely off. Now you're on your way to
developing your unexpected story.

~~~~~~~~~~~~~~~~~~~~~~~~~~~~~~

For example, I've mentioned before how my initial dream
was to be an actress. I went on a few open calls for children's roles in movies when I was very young. Then, in
fourth grade when my mom was in between full-time
jobs, I very briefly had an agent who would send me on
auditions in New York City. Now, I never booked anything,
because despite being five foot six in the fourth grade, I
was not a model-esque child. I was a weird-looking half
girl/half woman with no boobs and a lot of baby teeth that
were very late to fall out. I went on the crappiest auditions;
I remember auditioning for a print advertisement for
bathrobes and auditioning to be on a book cover for some
Sweet Valley Twins knockoff series. Then my mom got a

job and told me she couldn't take me into the city anymore for auditions, and my child acting and modeling career was over before it even began. I was hardly a "child star."

Somehow, as I aged, I concocted a memory that as a child I was in the movie *Rocky* in a small role, as "The Little Girl." I frequently told people this, starting around my college years. This was before anyone could whip out a smartphone and prove me wrong, so people just took my word for it, probably because I was always emphasizing what a small part it was.

After college, in my New York City days, I still talked about it. I would tell people that I didn't remember much about it but it was my first job. Still, everyone just took my word for it. Friends, casting directors, agents, dates . . . everyone was very impressed. Then I started to wonder why I had never taken the time to see the film *Rocky* if it was my big break. Understandably, at the age I played the role, it would have been an inappropriate movie to show me, but why didn't my parents own a copy of *Rocky* among their shelves full of VHS tapes? They had copies of movies I know they never watched, like *Boyz n the Hood* and *Carlito's Way*. Why wouldn't they purchase a copy of the movie that was their daughter's big break?

So at some point, I asked my mom about *Rocky*, wondering if I was more of a featured extra, or if I had a speaking part. My mom responded, "There was no little girl in *Rocky*. You went to a cattle call to play a little girl in a movie called *Ragtime*, and you didn't get the part. It went to director Mike Nichols's daughter. How long have you been telling people this? Why didn't anyone question you? How many people have you lied to?"

We had a good laugh, and I was proven very, very wrong. Not only was I not in the film *Rocky*, but also the part I'd concocted playing didn't even exist! To me, what's unexpected about this being-proven-wrong story is not that my mind rewrote a piece of my history (to my advantage) but that for about five or six years, everyone just took my word for it. They believed me when I said I played a role that didn't even exist in an Oscar-nominated film.*

Q: How do I know if I have really thrown an unexpected twist into my story? I know when something is funny, because people will laugh, but how can I gauge if something is unexpected?

A: When I was in a college acting class, my professor asked us to prepare a performance that would "change the breath" of our audience. Students did very unique things. One girl sprayed us with water in

---

* It makes me wonder what else I could get away with lying about.

TRY FOR AN

"OH NO SHE DIDN'T!"

REACTION FROM YOUR AUDIENCE RATHER THAN AN

"OF COURSE SHE DID!"

the middle of her presentation. We all had a vocal reaction to that. Someone else read a sickeningly sweet love poem that made us all ooh and aah. I told a funny story with a twist ending. I got gasps and laughs and audible "What the fucks." So I challenge you to change your audience's breath. Try and get a vocal reaction from them: a gasp, a shout, a sigh, a whimper, a laugh that goes on so long that it becomes a clap, a shout. These reactions signify that you have achieved the unexpected in your tale.

⋛ TELL YOUR STORY ⋛

Fill in this blank and repeat until you run out of memories.

I CAN'T BELIEVE I ONCE _____.

~~~~~~~~~~~~~~~~~~~~~~~~~~~~~~~~

This prompt will give you insight into ways you have surprised even yourself. If you were shocked by your actions, imagine how shocked an audience would be!

Beware of plot "twists" that your audience can easily predict.

Again, there are exceptions. Maybe you can make one of these feel new and fresh and surprise your audience. But why not challenge yourself to throw a few curveballs here

CLICHÉ ALERT

You thought you were going to be the teacher, but you ended up being the student. Been there, done that! Expected! We hear tales all the time of the volunteer who learns more from this new culture than the people of the culture learned from him/her.

You fall in love with someone you initially disliked. Okay, have you read *Pride and Prejudice*? Or watched *10 Things I Hate About You* (a.k.a. a modern *Taming of the Shrew*)? Or *Beauty and the Beast* or about a zillion other books and movies with this plotline?

Your story ends with you quitting the job you describe in detail as the greatest nightmare you have ever lived. Of course you quit! If you still worked there, you probably wouldn't be telling the story (see Chapter 8).

and there? One of my favorite stories to tell is about the year I tried to be an elementary school teacher and realized by the end of the year that I just didn't care enough to succeed at it. Audiences are always surprised at the twist of me *not* fighting to keep that cushy job in that story.

I just heard a fabulous story about two people growing up in the same hometown who hated each other. The guy asked the girl (the storyteller) out one night when she was driving him home. He said to her, "Either you agree to go on a date with me or you drive me back to the party." And the storyteller said, "And you bet I drove his ass right back to that party!" It got the whole crowd belly-laughing because it was unexpected, as opposed to the predictable "And I looked into his eyes, and realized then and there that it was true love."

Instead of the job you quit, I'd rather hear the story of the job you hate but can't seem to get fired from. Or the job that you think you're getting laid off from but instead keep getting promoted. Think of the hilarity that George's bigwig job at the New York Yankees brought to *Seinfeld*. It was so unpredictable that he would land such a dream job and continuously get promoted and complimented for the terrible job he was doing.

> *The best surprise parties are the ones when the guest of honor really had no idea. Think of the expression on that person's face. Now try and re-create that moment with your audience when you tell your tale.*

CHAPTER 14

THE BENIGN

Action-adventure, that genre, only
works for me if you can care about the
characters. If the hero's not taking some
kind of a journey, then there are no stakes—
and no stakes, then you don't care if he
lives, or dies, wins or loses.

**—BRANDON LEE,
actor and martial artist**

———————————

I spoke a lot about emotional investment in Chapter 6.
However, when the story is a really silly one, and you add
high stakes on top of deep passion, hilarity ensues.

PASSION + HIGH STAKES + "DUMB PLOT" = ROFL

> **GEORGE:** See, this should be a show. This is the show . . .
>
> **JERRY:** . . . Well, what's the show about?
>
> **GEORGE:** It's about nothing.
>
> —*SEINFELD* episode **"The Pitch"**

The hilarious TV show *Seinfeld* is often described as a show "about nothing." Many of its episodes tell a story using the Passion + High Stakes + "Dumb" Plot = ROFL formula. Here are some examples:

EPISODE: "THE SPONGE"

Passion: Elaine loves the Today sponge method of birth control.

High Stakes: It's going off the market, and Elaine only has a limited amount (one case) of Today sponges before she will *never* be able to get it ever again.

Dumb Plot: Elaine must decide if every man she is involved with from this moment forward is "sponge-worthy." She believes she only has sixty more times to have sex for the rest of her life, because if she runs out of the sponge she refuses to use other birth control options.

EPISODE: "THE COMEBACK"

Passion: George passionately loves his comeback to his coworker Reilly's public insult "Hey, George, the ocean called. They're running outta shrimp." (George was gulping down shrimp during a New York Yankees work meeting.) George's comeback is "The jerk store called, and they're running outta you." The only problem is, he thought of it after the fact.

High Stakes: George *must* get his revenge. He will stop at nothing.

Dumb Plot: George finds a way to fly to Akron, Ohio, and set the stage in a way that his jerk-store comeback will make sense at a company meeting at Reilly's new job at Firestone.

~~~~~~~~~~~~~~~~~~~~~~

Passion, your perspective (your spin on the situation), and high stakes can take a benign story and make it soar. You too can tell a story about the little things in life—a great muffin, a trip to the post office, the world's most boring day—and make it captivating and hilarious with simple tools. Ask yourself these questions to see if you may have a benign story to tell.

• Have you ever had an overly emotional reaction to something that now seems ridiculous? For example, have you ever cried in a laundromat? Cursed at customer service? Hugged a barista?

• Have you ever engaged in an argument that seems dumb now, but which at the time meant everything to you? Have you ever gotten into a serious fight over a board game? Have you argued over the proper way to baste a turkey? Gotten really getting heated up over a restaurant bill?

• Have you ever gone the distance to prove a point? Maybe you lost a bunch of weight to impress your high school crush at the reunion, only to go and discover he had gotten pretty chubby and didn't care. Did you save up all your money to buy an expensive item to prove that you're a grown-up, and then never even use it?

I have found myself riveted multiple times in the past by a student's quest for things that are obviously not life-or-death necessities, such as the perfect apartment, pair of shoes, couch, etc. If the stakes are high and the storyteller will stop at nothing to get what they want, I am in! A good example of this is the movie *Harold & Kumar Go to White Castle*. These guys aren't trying to save the world, but they have added high stakes to a silly quest.

TOOLS TO MAKE A BENIGN STORY ABOUT "NOTHING" POP

- **Set the stakes at the top.**

For example, I won a Moth storytelling competition with a story about Reese's Peanut Butter Cups. At these storytelling competitions, I have seen winning stories about amnesia, eating disorders, molestation, war, and every other very serious topic in the world. And somehow, my little story about candy took home the grand prize one night.

Here's why: I spent two minutes at the top of my story describing how much I loved not only Reese's Peanut Butter Cups but the holiday-edition peanut-butter cups. I'm talkin' the pumpkins, the trees, the hearts, and the eggs. I went into great detail about how superior they are to the regular cups, because: 1. They're all middle, no ridge; 2. They have a higher concentration of peanut butter to chocolate; 3. They're saltier; 4. *They are only available for a limited time.* Because I cannot get these candies for a large chunk of the year, meaning they are an exclusive item, just like Elaine's "Today Sponge," makes the stakes high.

- **Show us how much you care.**

Give examples of how far you have gone in terms of the subject of your benign/silly story. I once had a student tell a story of purchasing an additional suitcase on his way back from Seattle in order to bring home a case of a certain type of dish-washing sponge that was no longer available in his area in California.

In my Reese's story, I speak of racing to the Rite Aid the day after Valentine's Day to pick up the half-price peanut-butter hearts before I am faced with the full-priced peanut-butter Easter eggs as my only option for deliciousness. I also discuss how when the hearts come around, I know that there will soon be only eggs left before we go into what I call "the period of darkness," which is the time from April to October where no holiday edition Reese's are available.

- **Tell us what happened regarding the dumb thing you care about.**

A story is just a rant unless you get to the meat of it. You can certainly spend time up top setting the stakes and showing us how much you care, but you must eventually get to the middle, or the "meat" of your story. Otherwise, your story is all introduction. Think of the middle of your story as the peanut butter center of the Reese's cup. That's what you really want to get to. The chocolate coating (or the ridged exterior if you are buying the non-holiday edition Reese's)* is simply there to bookend the main event,

---

* But why would you?

the peanut butter. The middle of your story should have a plot. It's the part of the story where you dive into a specific event that happened and the audience really starts to root for you on your journey.

So, in my Reese's story, I then dive into the story of getting a call from my mother telling me that my favorite aunt passed away, and then wanting to soothe my pain by emotionally eating my favorite candy in the world, only to discover that my husband had eaten all of my Reese's hearts.

• **Tell us how irrationally you reacted to said dumb thing you care about.**

Remember, we root for you if you are flawed! We love emotional reactions to anything, whether you're crying with joy because you just got engaged or sobbing to an old woman at a laundromat when your favorite sweater got bleach all over it. I'll never forget the student who told the story of her favorite black jacket. She set the stage about how much she loved it, going back to the day she first saw it on the rack, and telling all the places and occasions she's worn it. She smiled ear to ear speaking of it. Then she dove into a story of her car getting broken into while she was at the park with her daughters. The audience was in hysterics when the storyteller admitted that her first instinct was to run directly into the crime scene, destroying evidence in the process, to see if her black jacket was still in the car. When she didn't even notice she'd lost sight of her daughters in the chaos, we were so on board with her we laughed even harder. At the point in the story where her husband rushed over with her daughters, all she said was, "My jacket! They didn't take my jacket! It's okay!" Meanwhile, many other valuables had been taken and her daughters narrowly escaped getting lost, but we were still on this storyteller's side because she set the stakes at the top and showed us how much she cared. Without diving into the story of the day her car got broken into, this story would simply be a list of reasons why she liked her black jacket.

Back to my Reese's story, I, too, reacted irrationally when I discovered my candies were missing, calling my husband at his job, yelling and crying to him, and threatening that he would really be in trouble if he couldn't get his hands on some half-price hearts, *not* full-price eggs, before I saw him that night. (The subtext of this, of course, is that I am actually upset over my aunt but channeling it all into chocolate.)

- **Have a sense of humor about it all.**

Don't get angry when recalling the story. Instead, try laughing about yourself. Emotional reactions are important, and can often drive a story, but I have seen people get so worked up during a story that I feel like I am being

yelled at. I want to be entertained, not scolded. So don't
be afraid to poke fun at yourself for filling a suitcase with
dish-washing sponges, putting your jacket's safety above
your own children's safety, or yelling at your husband over
holiday candy. Throw in phrases like "I had truly gone to
the dark side" or "I knew I was crossing a line, but I didn't
care," to make us more on board. Lines like that show
us that you realize you are being crazy/silly/irrational.
Without acknowledging this, you risk the audience wondering whether they should call you a psychiatrist at the
end of your piece.

- **At the end of your story, give us a little
zinger, showing us that you still care about the
"dumb" thing.**

This can be done in the form of a cute tag or PS, to drive
home your piece, e.g., "I'm running out of dish-washing
sponges—good thing I hear Seattle is beautiful this time
of year" or "Recently I saw my favorite jacket was back
on the racks at the Gap. I snatched up two more just in
case." Or for me, in my Reese's story I said, "Thank God
my aunt passed away during the window between half-
priced hearts/full-priced eggs. Because I don't know how I
would have handled it if she had left us during the 'period
of darkness.'"

You know . . . my favorite stories are true stories from our lives. Stories about us just living in the world together.

—SPALDING GRAY,
Morning, Noon and Night

⋚ TELL YOUR STORY ⋚

Try to show exactly who you are as a person through a benign story. Do your best to make a story about "nothing" pop.

For inspiration, check out Spalding Gray's book *Morning, Noon and Night*, in which he recounts a day in his life with his three kids in Sag Harbor, New York. It's a monologue essentially about nothing. Yet I zipped through it in one day.

PART 3

the

PERFORMANCE
AND BEYOND

CHAPTER 15

HOW TO MEMORIZE & VOCALIZE A STORY

That simultaneous joy of creating something and sharing it with an audience—it's the same now as it was then, when it was just my cousins' birthday party.

—STEVE BUSCEMI,
actor and director

Preparing a story for a performance/presentation/conference/etc. is not just as simple as writing it down and reading it aloud. Just so you have it all in one place, here are some tricks I've mentioned before to keep in mind when preparing your tale.

STORYTELLING GUIDELINES

- Keep it true.
- Change names and identifying characteristics of other people in your story if you feel it's necessary.
- Make sure your story has a universal theme that is relatable, not self-indulgent or overly personal.
- Have multiple points of entry.
- Don't be heavy-handed with your message. Let the story speak for itself.
- If you're not "over it," don't tell it.
- Tell us what you were thinking at the time of your story. Reveal your inner monologue, from A to Z.
- Cut the fat when introducing external characters. Use composite characters and nickname them when you can.
- Make sure we root for you. Be an underdog.
- Show us your flaws and use them to your advantage when telling your story.
- If there are full-circle connections within your story, be sure to use them. But don't force a connection.
- Be the star of your story.

• Add nostalgia (songs, television shows, fashion styles from the time of the story).

• Keep us on our toes by incorporating the unexpected.

• Keep it conversational, not presentational. Cut out anything you wouldn't say to a group of your friends. You want your story to sound natural.

• Make sure you aren't just listing things, going on a rant, or making a political speech. Make sure you get to the "meat" of the story.

• If you care, we care. Passion will take you far. Emotionally respond to the tale you are recounting, but don't yell at us!

Keeping these elements in mind, I am a strong believer in writing your story out word for word first. I don't mean an outline, or a series of notes; I mean a written piece. But don't write this as if it is to be published in a magazine or book. No one will see this but you. Write it exactly the way you would actually say it out loud if you were to tell it to a group of friends. Use your own slang/abbreviations/etc. when writing the story how you would speak it. Don't complicate it.*

---

* Note: You won't be memorizing your story word for word, but more on that later.

There is no need to include phrases like "'I'll do it myself,' my sister said with a sneer." In storytelling, you can just write, "Then my sister said, 'I'll do it myself.'" In your delivery, you can convey that she said it with a sneer by changing the tone of your voice and your facial expression. Basically, eliminate anything in the family of "she exclaimed," "my father angrily contested," "my daughter whispered," "cackled my stepbrother," and so on. All of that can be *shown* within the performance of your story. Spelling it out just slows your piece down. Fancy explanations are unnecessary.

Some descriptions of how you feel about certain things can also be shown in the performance. I know I have stressed how important it is to *tell* your audience your stance or opinion on the events you are recalling, but why not shake it up a few times in your story, and let your delivery show us how you feel?

I once had a student who told a story of a bad online dating experience. In the first minute of her story, she had the line "So I decided to try online dating." I asked her how she felt about that. Was she excited to search for a mate on the Internet? Or was it a bit of a letdown to pursue love electronically? She said she was really unhappy about trying it at first. So I told her to simply say "online dating" in the tone she felt about it. In her performance, she got a huge laugh when she said, "So I decided to try [sigh, lower voice] online dating."

I call this technique stressing "product words." When you see a commercial, usually the actor will say the name of the product in a different way than the rest of the commercial script, as to emphasize its importance and let us know how much he or she likes it. For example, "And that's why I use . . . *Excedrin PM*."

Look at the product words in your piece, whether they are things you like (e.g., holiday-edition Reese's Peanut Butter Cups) or things you dislike (e.g., online dating). It doesn't have to actually be a "product," just something you have an opinion on.

STEPS FOR WRITING YOUR STORY

1. Intro: Begin your story. Remember the tricks of starting your tale with "So," or with a thesis statement. No need for a grandiose intro that you would never in a million years say when causally recounting this tale for friends. Start with just some basic info about you that pertains to the tale you are about to tell. It's not necessary to tell us everything about yourself; just stick to stuff that is vital for us to know before you really get into this story. This usually ends up being just a brief paragraph. However, it can also be a few quick anecdotes exemplifying that you are "terrified of heights" or whatever the meat of your story is, e.g., "I have hidden in the bathroom of many a rooftop party in my day. I once pretended I had hives to get out of a church rock-climbing retreat."

2. Middle/"Meat": This is where you dive into a specific event that changed or affected you in some way. This part will have conflict, whether within yourself or with another person/force. It should build to a climax leading to some sort of resolution.

3. Conclusion: You don't want to end your piece with "And then I stepped to the edge of the cliff . . . Thank you. Good night." We're going to want to know what happened next: "And then I stepped to the edge of the cliff, spread my wings, and began to do something the old me would have never done. I was hang-gliding!" And then we want a little resolution: "As the wind hit my face, I forgot all about the things I'd been missing out on my whole life. I was ready to move forward." Remember, don't tell us the moral of the story. Don't spell out what you learned. Some options for a conclusion are:

- Just tell us what happened next: "It was over before I knew it. My feet hit the ground, and I walked right back into the hang-gliding office and scheduled my next adventure."

• End on a laugh: "I was ready to move forward, right up until the moment I threw up in my mouth. But hey, at least I was cool for about thirty seconds."

• End your story where you began. If you're stuck about how to end your piece, it often helps to go back and look at the first paragraph. There might be a phrase in there you can repeat to bring your piece full circle: "So a few weeks later I got an invite to a rooftop party, and without even thinking about it, I replied with an enthusiastic yes. This time, I may even make it out of the bathroom and onto that rooftop."

4. Tag/PS (optional): A tag should only be used if you have an organic (not forced or Googled) update about the events/people in your story. Something like "By the way, my birthday was last week and my parents gave me a two-hundred-dollar gift card. Does anyone know how much it costs to go hang-gliding these days?" Or "I recently bumped into my pastor—the one I lied to about having hives to get out of his rock-climbing retreat. When I saw him, I asked, 'Have any more rock-climbing retreats coming up? I think my hives have finally cleared up. And by "hives," I mean "crippling fear of heights." He told me he'd 'be in touch.'"*

It's important for you to read your story out loud, rather than to have a friend read it on the page. You will be telling this story, and there are quirks that only you can make come alive when reading it out loud. Your story risks falling (falsely) flat when just read on the page.

Don't ask too many people for their insights, just one or two people whose opinions you trust. Otherwise, your head will be spinning with conflicting opinions and you will start to doubt your whole piece. For actors, or friends of actors, I like to use a headshot analogy. When an actor gets new professional photos ("headshots") taken, it's common for the actor to get opinions from friends about which shots are best. That actor should ask very few people, and only those whose opinions are coming from an educated place as to what would work best professionally. Often actors make the mistake of asking everyone they know, or even posting all the pictures on social media and asking all one thousand of their closest "friends" to choose the best shot. What ends up happening is that everyone

---

* I know it's tempting, but like I said in Chapter 11, it's usually best not to force a PS by Googling someone. The best stories happen in real life. If you have no real-life update, just end your story at the conclusion.

AFTER YOU'VE WRITTEN the FIRST DRAFT of YOUR STORY, PUT IT DOWN. DON'T EDIT OR JUDGE IT. INSTEAD, WAIT a DAY OR TWO, THEN READ IT OUT LOUD to A FRIEND will pick a different favorite photo and the actor will have no idea which photo is best and be more confused than if he/she had asked no one in the first place. So streamline the list of people you show your work to. Also be sure to choose people who will give you honest feedback, not just inflate your ego and tell you how awesome you are (although that's nice too).

GOOD THINGS TO ASK YOUR SUPPORTIVE FRIEND TO LOOK FOR:

1. Was it easy to follow? Were you confused by anything?
2. Did you root for me?
3. Could you keep all my characters straight?
4. Did you relate?

After you get some notes, make whatever revisions are necessary. Then look at your story again and identify the universal theme. Write that at the top of your piece, but don't tell anyone what it is.

After you've identified the universal theme, you'll then break up your story into memorizable chunks. So while

YOUR UNIVERSAL THEME IS *LIKE THE* BIRTHDAY WISH *YOU MAKE* WHEN YOU BLOW OUT YOUR CANDLES—

IT WOULD CHEAPEN THE MOMENT FOR YOU TO ANNOUNCE TO YOUR FRIENDS WHAT IT IS this story if published might only be six paragraphs, when broken up into memorizable chunks it could be eighteen paragraphs. Remember, no one is seeing this but you, so don't worry about proper punctuation, grammar and spelling. These chunks should each be identified as "the part of my story when ..." something happens.

So maybe your chunks could be separated into some version of this:

1. The part of my story when I introduce myself and my fear of heights

2. The part of my story when I dive into examples of previous ways I've avoided heights

3. The part of my story when I start dating a girl I want to impress and go into detail about how much I like her

4. The part of my story when she invites me to go hang-gliding

And so on ...

Once you've broken your piece down into these chunks, underline the product words, and then go into the margins of your paper and write the most essential moments you need to hit in each chunk. If there is a vital detail, funny joke, character intro, or plot point, be sure to make a note of that in the margin. Take this story chunk, for example:

"And then I stepped to the edge of the cliff, spread my wings, and began to do something the old me would have never done. I was hang-gliding! As the wind hit my face, I forgot all about the things I'd been missing out on my whole life. I was ready to move forward."

The notes in your margin may read "step to edge," "wings," "wind in face," "move forward."

Next, go to a notebook and write down quick words or phrases to help you remember your story in order. This should take up about one to two pages depending on the length of your story. I call it a "beat sheet," but those of you who are musicians or stand-up comedians may think it resembles a "set list."

Going back to the hang-gliding story, here's how your beat sheet may look:

- Fear of heights
- Hives/rooftop/rock climbing
- Meeting Sarah at her b-day party
- Cool girl—impress her
- Third date—hang-gliding
- Inner monologue—why I should cancel
- Fears of Sarah dumping me if I don't hang-glide
- Inner monologue—Sarah is the one!
- Arrive at hang-glide place/equipment

- Hike up mountain
- Inner monologue—watching Sarah go first
- Hesitation to jump
- Hang-gliding terror—then peace, wind on face
- Landing—Sarah kiss
- Returning equipment—scheduling next hang-glide
- Running into rooftop party guy—all good

Before you present your story, review your beat sheet, not your fully written piece. I am a strong believer in not memorizing a story word for word, but instead by what happened next. And because you lived this story, you know exactly what happened next. I have seen close to zero students in all my years of teaching forget their story onstage due to this method.

So let's review the steps:

1. Write draft of your story word for word.
2. Ask a friend or two for notes.
3. Revise.
4. Identify the universal theme and write it on top.
5. Break up the story into memorizable chunks.
6. Underline the product words.
7. Write notes in the margins of things to remember.
8. Narrow those things down further into a beat sheet.
9. Familiarize yourself with the beat sheet.
10. Hit the stage!

IF YOUR STORY DOESN'T GO SO WELL THE FIRST TIME YOU PERFORM IT, DON'T THROW IT AWAY & LABEL IT A "BAD STORY"

So now that you've lived your story, written it out, revised it, broken it into chunks, written notes in the margins, written a beat sheet—there is no way you're not ready to present it. Simply review your beat sheet, then put it down and hit the stage, boardroom, podium, whatever! Preparing a story by this method can make you look like you are so charming and brilliant that you have just come up with this fabulous story on the spot. It will differ ever so slightly every time you tell it. However, you will minimize tangents/rambling, hit all the important parts you need to hit, and stay on point to reach the ending of your story.

There are lots of reasons a story may fall flat at first. Maybe your nerves got in the way. Perhaps you rushed through it so you didn't run over time. Maybe your story needs a few more revisions. Perhaps it just wasn't the right story for that crowd? None of these are reasons to give up. Everyone has bombed at some point. Legend has it that Bob Dylan was booed onstage the first time he plugged in a guitar rather than sticking with his usual acoustic set. But other versions of this story claim that only half the audience booed; the other half was cheering. And it's pretty safe to say his career went on.

The first time I performed the Reese's Peanut Butter Cup story I referenced in Chapter 14 was in a variety show.

This show was not specifically a storytelling show, but I figured it would be pretty story-friendly. Boy, was I wrong. My story bombed so hard that when I walked offstage my friend sitting next to me said, "Don't quit the business over this. Stick with it." He could see on my face I was contemplating a whole other career path—it was that bad.

A few weeks later, I went to a Moth StorySLAM where the theme was "Good Food." I had prepared my story about choking on the steak and getting Heimliched by a distant relative of Dr. Heimlich, as referenced in Chapter 8. The show began, I put my name in the hat (this was an open-mic story slam where ten names get chosen out of the hat to tell a story), and the host launched into a story of choking on her food in a restaurant and having to receive the Heimlich maneuver. The crowd loved it! All I could think was, "Oh my God—I can't get picked! If I do, I'll be telling a version of her story right after her and I'll totally bomb this!" Then I racked my brain to see if I had any other food-related stories to fit the theme. All I had was that sucky Reese's Peanut Butter Cup story that had made me want to quit storytelling. And just as I calmed myself down about how many times I had been to these competitions and *not* been chosen out of the hat, the host called my name.

I had no choice but to do the story I had written off as the worst story ever. Except, this time, at a show that was specifically a storytelling show, with a different crowd—a crowd that was excited to hear stories about food—my Reese's story killed. I had laughs the whole way through. I won the competition, telling the exact same story I had told and bombed with at the variety show, and I was later contacted by an NPR show that wanted to play the story on the air. Had I thrown that story out after the first time, I would have never known how far it could soar. So give yourself a break and don't expect perfection immediately.*

Q: How do you feel about bringing a script/beat sheet/notes of any kind onstage?

A: In the storytelling shows that I have produced, I have a "no notes, no scripts" clause. I think there is something magical about watching a person tell, not read, a story. However, there are other shows that prefer that you read your story word for word. There are also shows that don't mind if you bring up notes. I like to simply tell my story. Have I brought notes up onstage? Sure— especially when something is brand-new, or for the shows I did in the months after I had a baby.**

---

* That advice is intended more for me than you.
** Note to self: If I have another baby, put money aside for those night nurses I keep hearing about so I can get some sleep and function as a human being!

I'm only human, and so are you. So you be the judge of whether or not you bring notes up. But when my students present stories for an audience at the end of their classes, they do not use notes, and they rock it, remembering their stories fully, without blanking. All they have to remember is what happened next, rather than what their next line is. And they always remember what happened next, because it's their life, and they lived it.*

Q: I don't want to write anything. I think my story will be better if I just get up and tell it. What do you think?

A: I beg to differ. I am speaking from years of teaching and performing experience—don't just wing it. Have I ever winged it? Sure, a few times here and there, but only a handful of times in a pinch, and only after years of teaching and hundreds of live performances under my belt. And the stories I winged it with fell a lot flatter than the stories I prepared.

I have had many students fight me on this. But I am not asking you to write your life story. I'm asking you to write one true story from your life. In my classes that story

---

* See—now it makes even more sense why your story needs to be true!

needs to be only five to six minutes. That's roughly two and a half pages. That's not much. I am not asking you to memorize that, just remember the main components. You won't be able to whittle that down if you don't write it out. I once had a student go so far as to insist on not writing, even as we prepped for our final class performance. Now, this was in my first year or two of teaching, so I told her that if she really didn't want to write, she didn't have to. She could just wing it for the performance. Now, after teaching for many years, I would tell her if she didn't write her story she couldn't participate in the final performance, but you live and learn, right?

Well, I am really glad I let her slide, because it was a nice experiment. Everyone else in the class took the necessary steps to prepare their story, and their stories soared in the show. However, when the student who refused to write presented her piece, it ran over the time limit, had no real ending, went on a number of unnecessary tangents, and— to put it bluntly—was kind of a disaster.

So that's what happens when a person new to storytelling just wings it. It doesn't work.

I once had a lovely student who was an actor. After class he said to me, "I'm used to memorizing lines and monologues word for word in my acting work, so I think it would work better for me to memorize my story word for word for the show. Is that okay?" I told him I didn't recommend it, but if it made him more comfortable onstage, then okay. As long as he was prepared and felt confident, I figured he would do well.

The day of the show, this student told his story and killed it. He got laughs in all the right places, held the audience's attention, and seemed, most importantly, like he was having fun telling it. After the show, humbled by the whole experience, I congratulated him. This student had gone rogue, used his own method—one I advise against—and rocked it. The teacher had become the student. When I hugged him, he said, "Oh, by the way, memorizing word for word was too much work. I used the beat-sheet method instead." Aha! The teacher remains the teacher!

> While some others pray, I narrate and then I save it.
> **—SPALDING GRAY**

Q: What has been the response to your students who have prepared stories this way?

A: Dozens of my former students have won the Moth StorySLAM competition by preparing stories this way. Many have gone on to win the title of Moth GrandSLAM champion (where recent winners of city-wide slams compete for one grand prize). I have even been beaten a number of times in these competitions by former students. Many of my students from corporate classes have switched to prepping their business presentations this way and had greater success in their careers. A number of my former students have been selected to do TED talks and used this method to prepare. I could go on and on about the pride I have in my former students and all they have accomplished, but I should stop gushing now. What I'm trying to say is, there's a reason I decided to write a book on this method, so trust me and try it. It works.

CHAPTER 16

THE BUSINESS OF STORYTELLING

Weird doors open. People fall into things.
Maybe the engineering whiz will wind up
brewing cider, not because he has to but
because he finds it challenging. Who knows?

**—DAVID SEDARIS, "What I Learned,"
as published in the *New Yorker***

The truth is, it really doesn't matter what business
opportunities storytelling gets you. What matters is that
you share your truth. If sharing that truth leads to some
exciting opportunities, my advice would be to say yes to

things that scare you, be flexible with your plan of where you want things to take you,* and be grateful for whatever opportunities arise. I certainly am.

That being said, great storytelling is obviously useful in a variety of situations, such as a professional presentation, a wedding speech, a eulogy, a first date, an audition, or a job interview. In fact, most of the people who enroll in my storytelling classes are not aspiring writers, actors, or comedians, but doctors, lawyers, scientists, teachers, web developers, restaurant owners, and business leaders hoping to present more effectively. Storytelling is essential when it comes to the business world. Even if you're not making presentations, it's invaluable to network well in order to succeed in your field, and networking is largely fueled by . . . storytelling!

People often talk about how well Bill Clinton can remember specific aspects of people's lives, even years after he's seen them. As in "Hello, Susan. How did that new recipe for those chocolate-chip cookies turn out?" Granted, this is part of Clinton's charm and helpful in getting him where he is today. But the other side of the coin is "Susan," who might have told Clinton a story about how

---

* Remember, I wanted to be a stage actress when I first graduated from college.

she liked to bake. Stories are far more memorable than just a statement of fact. And when networking, unless you say something memorable, you can easily be forgotten.

This played out in my own life quite recently, when I took a general meeting at a large television studio. When the executive mentioned she had just gotten back from Africa, we chatted about her experiences visiting ancestral lands. I told her that my son is very large and fair and I wondered if we might have some Viking ancestry, and that I was so curious I'd just taken an ancestry DNA test and was waiting for the results. A month later, when I was called back in to that same television studio for a second meeting, the executive admitted, "I half called you in because I wanted to know the results of your ancestry test."*

On the first day of every class I teach, whether that class is full of twenty-two-year-old writers or forty-five-year-old ad executives, I always give them the same first exercise.

> Tell me something odd/interesting/unique
> about you. This should not be so personal
> that you would only tell a therapist, but
> also not so safe that it will bore us all (e.g.,
> "My fun fact is, I love coffee"). Try to find

---

* Spoiler alert: I am *not* a Viking.

something in the middle, such as "I am an identical twin," "I've been to all fifty states," or "I used to dance competitively."

Note how all the examples are actually conversation starters. "Oh, you're an identical twin. How many minutes are you apart? Who was born first? Do you feel like the 'older' sibling because you're four minutes older?" Already, by revealing a small personal thing, you have made yourself memorable. And in any business, being memorable is half the battle.

> *You'll stand out from the crowd if you can talk about yourself in an engaging manner.*

Once you have your go-to fun facts for networking, I suggest you take it a step further and develop go-to stories. Only you can be the judge as to which stories are appropriate for a business setting. Believe me, I'm the queen of TMI.

Q: Why would I need a go-to story for business?

A: Because it will make you more likable.
Here's the thing. I would love to live in a world where the most qualified candidate gets ahead based on

credentials and accomplishments alone, but that's simply not the reality. Many business decisions are made simply because a decision maker liked one person over the other. Especially in hiring, the decision maker thinks, "Would I want to spend forty-plus hours a week with this person?" If you can win over a new boss/a potential client/an agent/ etc. by making him/her laugh or root for you with your personal story, you'll be more likely to get ahead.

> *Decision makers often choose the candidate they like personally. Don't give up an opportunity to let your personality shine.*

≳ TELL YOUR STORY ≲

How did you get started in the business you're in? Think back to how it all began, and how you first became interested in it.

What did you originally think you wanted to do? Fun fact: In *This American Life* episode 202 titled "Plan B," host Ira Glass asked about 100 people "to remember back to when they first hit adulthood. What is it that they thought their lives would be like? What was their Plan A back then? And I asked them, OK, how many of you are still on Plan A? Out of 100 people, only one person raised her hand. Just one. The youngest person in the room. Just 23 years old. Everybody else in the room was like, Plan B? What about Plan C and D and F?"

Did you run into any obstacles while you were trying to get where you are today?

What is a specific story of success in your field that drives you to do what you do? A customer that really affected you? A small business you were able to offer a loan to? A family you were able to find the perfect home for?

~~~~~~~~~~~~~~~~~~~~~~~~~~~~~

In business meetings with someone new, you might be asked, "How did you get into this field?" It's a common enough question, and most people answer it directly, e.g., "Well, I majored in literature, so working in a library was a natural progression." Why not think of an interesting anecdote that got you where you are today? This can become your "origin story."

Admitting struggles along the way is usually okay in a business setting, especially if your anecdotes reflect an admirable personality trait. Stories of overcoming obstacles only make people want to work with you more. There's a perception that someone who has had everything handed to them may be less hardworking than someone who fought their way to the top.*

I recently had a student tell a hilarious origin story about how she became an media executive. She had majored in forensic psychology, thinking she would be like Clarice Starling from *The Silence of the Lambs*. However, after she got placed working in a juvenile detention center, she quickly discovered that she didn't like working in the field. In her own hilarious words she said, "I discovered I didn't like helping other people with their problems." She then tried temping for a while and ended up on a long-term assignment for a company that wanted to hire her full-time. When they offered her the job, she asked her potential new boss, "What exactly is it that you do here?" It turns out she had basically been doing nothing for months and her temp agency had never explained what the assignment was. She took the job, which led her to a career in media/advertising. "But don't worry," she said. "I still use my forensic psychology degree every day when dealing with my clients." Do you see how much more memorable this ad executive is compared to someone who

---

* In fact, when I was in college, there was a rumor that Juilliard graduates were intentionally overlooked by casting directors when entering the real world of auditioning, just to give them a dose of reality.

could only say, "I temped at an ad agency for a while and eventually went full-time?"

To better acquaint yourself with the quick, interesting kind of origin story I'm talking about, I'm going to once again direct you to *Shark Tank*. The credit sequence introduces the "Sharks" (the investors) and gives the quick story of how they got where they are. For example, "Barbara Corcoran turned a thousand-dollar loan into a five-billion-dollar real estate empire." Additionally, the Sharks often talk about their own personal stories as a way to connect with entrepreneurs. Mark Cuban mentions being a door-to-door salesman. Robert Herjavec speaks about his immigrant father, who worked in a factory. These successful businesspeople are open about their struggles along the way, which invests us more deeply with their show.

FIND COMMON GROUND

Before a business meeting or interview, it's always a good idea to research the person you are meeting with to see if you have anything in common, or even better to tell a story about something you have in common. I once did some research on a television executive before I met with him and discovered that he was a trivia buff who had once been on a game show. I also love trivia and have been on a game show, so I was able to connect with him about those things right away.

Later, when the executive is leafing through the résumés of the candidates, he won't be wondering, "Who was this person again?" but "Oh, yes, this person met her husband at a bar trivia night and was on *The Price Is Right*." Sometimes the slightest things make you stand out.

WHAT TO DO IF YOU'RE SHY

If you are particularly nervous about telling a story about yourself in a business setting, try putting the shoe on the other foot and getting stories out of others. It might put you in a position to create an organic conversation that leads to a long-term connection. This is a skill that's fun to practice. When getting your hair cut, don't just sit there on your smartphone; engage with your hairdresser. I once asked a hairdresser how long she'd worked at the salon. "Twenty years," she told me. I said that was a very long time to work at the same place. She said, "Oh, they'll never fire me." She then launched into a tear-jerking story about giving a woman a new hairstyle one day and deciding, because the salon was slow, to also do her makeup. When she spun the woman around to look at herself, the woman cried in joy, saying, "I never knew I could look this beautiful." The next day the woman called the salon owner to thank my hairdresser for saving her life. Turns out the woman had been contemplating suicide, but the hairdresser reminded her of the beauty she had within her, and she changed her mind.

> *Every person has a story. Engage with others. Get off your phone! Every person you meet is an opportunity to learn about a world you're not a part of.*

Exterminators, clients, waiters, flight attendants, and police officers—basically every person with a job has a story of the most extreme situation they've ever encountered in the workplace. The next time you find yourself interacting with a service provider, try getting a story out of them so you can put your skills into practice. They might even teach you a thing or two about how to respond when put on the spot.

QUESTIONS THAT ENCOURAGE STORYTELLING

• How long have you worked here? Do you like it? What makes you like it?
• What did you do before this?
• What made you become a _____?
• What is the weirdest thing that ever happened to you at work?
• What was the best thing that ever happened to you/that you ever witnessed at work?

STORYTELLING IN BUSINESS PRESENTATIONS

We all know our nerves can get the best of us during presentations. I encourage you to try to find a way to relax and center yourself beforehand. I do not suggest reviewing your notes up to the last second before you present. Instead, prepare early, put your notes down, and take some deep breaths. I always say to my students, "There is nothing in those notes that isn't in your brain already. Cramming at the last minute will just make you less focused." Also, right before you speak, take a very deep breath. If you watch any of my stories on YouTube, you will see me take a visible and audible deep breath right there on the stage before I start my performance. Believe me—it works!

Many of us have watched Don Draper and company woo a client with a personal story on *Mad Men*. Countless times. The client is unsure, and then Don says something like "When I was a little boy, I wanted to play baseball with the local kids, but I didn't have enough money for a glove. So I set up a lemonade stand to raise the money. It took three weeks, but finally I raised enough to get myself a glove at the five-and-dime. I wore that glove into the ground; we played baseball in the street every day that summer. It was the best summer of my life. Now, whenever I taste Minute Maid lemonade, it makes me think of those childhood summers that seemed endless."

And bam! The client is sold.

I encourage you to incorporate a personal story into almost any professional presentation. If you think Don Draper is the only one who does this, think again. Watch any cooking show, and notice how during the demonstration, star chefs like Giada De Laurentiis and Emeril Lagasse are always relaying a personal story, like "I used to eat chicken potpie whenever I was home sick from school. I know most people have chicken soup, but in my house it was chicken potpie. I even faked sick a few times just to get it. Now I make it all the time, no matter how I'm feeling."

Imagine that same cooking demonstration with simple narration of the steps, with dead air in between. You would change the channel instantly. In fact, once you are aware of this trick, you will notice everyone from doctors to teachers using personal stories to prove a point in *their* presentations.

> *A personal story can get the audience on your side before you launch into the meat of your presentation.*

Instead of telling your personal story, you can tell the story of a product, or a company. There are many businesses known for their origin stories. Two childhood friends started Ben & Jerry's. We all know that Facebook was created by a young Harvard dropout named Mark Zuckerberg. (That business origin story was so interesting it produced an Oscar-winning film.) We all associate KFC with Colonel Sanders, a man who started the global empire at age sixty-five while living off of $105 checks from social security. These aren't just businesses—we have faces and stories to associate with them. All of these business owners—hippies in Vermont, a college drop-out, a struggling retiree—are underdogs in their own ways, and all have benefitted tremendously from making their company origin story public. In a way, with every pint of ice cream we buy, every post we "like," and every piece of chicken we eat, we feel like we are a part of an underdog's success.

If you were to present new software for a dating website, why not remind everyone why the website was founded in the first place? Were the creators lucky or unlucky in love? Was that what inspired them to start their company? If you've created a tool that helps businesses, is there a specific success story you can share about your clientele before moving into your technical presentation? How can you make it even more personal? For example, "This new function is so easy even my mom could use it—and she still hasn't figured out how to use her DVR. The other day she asked me what part of the DVR does she put the tape in. Seriously, even she can do it." Now your audience knows a little about you, hopefully they relate, and they'll be more likely to pay attention to the rest of your presentation.

If you don't have a story about your specific product, why not? Are you fully engaging with it, and do you use it in your own life? I often talk about "living for the story," so if you don't have a story or memory about something you're selling, why not actively create one? Or go get those stories out of your clients?

> If you're going to try, go all the way. Otherwise, don't even start. This could mean losing girlfriends, wives, relatives and maybe even your mind. And, you'll do it, despite rejection and the worst odds. And it will be better than anything else you can imagine. If you're going to try, go all the way. There is no other feeling like that. You will be alone with the gods, and the nights will flame with fire. You will ride life straight to perfect laughter. It's the only good fight there is.
>
> **—CHARLES BUKOWSKI,**
> *Factotum**

There are no limits to where a good story can take you, personally or professionally.

You can even transform the actual craft of storytelling into a career. However, like any artistic endeavor you are passionate about, understand that it takes time and that you may not follow the exact path you expect.

---

* This was the novel that inspired me to give it my all and really focus on writing and storytelling. It's a fantastic book I could quote all day.

To "go all the way" it doesn't have to mean you must quit your job, have no way to pay your bills, and have nothing else going on in your life but your craft. Bukowski's thought is romantic, and from what I have read about his life, pretty truthful, but these are modern times and every person has different responsibilities. My interpretation is to commit to what you love, and take that as far as you can go, even if "as far as you can go" is learning about storytelling by listening to podcasts en route to work and back every day. There will be setbacks along the way to becoming a great storyteller.* But the rewards will be endless.

> Harvard undergraduates believe that inventing a job is better than finding a job.
>
> **—LARRY SUMMERS to the Winklevoss twins in *The Social Network***

When I graduated from college,** I didn't even know that storytelling was a thing. So, lucky you! You are many

---

* Remember, I almost quit after my now-award-winning Reese's story bombed the first time!

** Not from Harvard—not that you even thought that for a second, but just clarifying.

steps ahead of me when I started out. Not only do you know it's a "thing," you've just read a book about it, you have access to live storytelling online and through podcasts, and you may even live somewhere where you can see storytelling live and try it yourself.

Storytelling is so popular right now that you have a ready-made audience. Believe me, you are miles ahead of the resources I had when I began storytelling. Now is the perfect time to embark on your storytelling journey. So ... here are some ways you can pursue this craft and maybe even monetize it.

1. Start your own storytelling show.

Does your city/town have a storytelling night? If not, why not start one? You can make a cut of the door and already you are making money at this. If your town already has a storytelling night, good! Then there is demand. Give 'em a little competition.

To start, you'll need a name, and maybe a specialty. It's easier to market a storytelling show if it's called something more than just *Stories*. For example, former students of mine began a show called *The Story Collider*, which features science-related stories. Now it's a podcast, magazine, and internationally touring show.* So think of what you like hearing stories about and create your show from there.

2. Try and get your written stories published.

Sure, there are differences between writing for the stage and writing for the page, but the tools you have just from reading this book will set you way ahead of people just staring blankly at their laptop screens. Many of my students have published stories in the *Los Angeles Times*, *New York Press*, *Glamour* magazine, and more. You won't make millions—but you may make a little, and you'll help build your platform toward bigger-paying gigs.

3. Write your memoir and try to get it published.

I know this sounds easier said than done, but I have had a few really driven students get their books sold. These books have contained true stories that they worked on in class. A word of advice: it's best to figure out the overarching theme to your life ("the story of your life") and group the stories under some sort of umbrella, to help market them. It's easier to sell *Jacob's Book of Drunken College Stories* than *Jacob's Life*. For example, my former student Selena Coppock, was able to package her stories under

---

* Two of these fabulous award-winning and published storytellers were shy physicists, by the way.

the umbrella of her life as a blonde, and sold her book, *The New Rules for Blondes: Highlights from a Fair-Haired Life*, to HarperCollins. It's possible!

4. Start a podcast.

Yes, there are many storytelling podcasts already, but that doesn't mean you can't put your unique spin on it. Just like for a live show, try and find a theme for your podcast. This is an already oversaturated market, so you really want to stand out. Just think about what type of stories you would be interested in hearing, and there's your answer. And you can expand to live tours or a distribution deal. The sky's the limit with this growing, very story-friendly form.

5. Link your stories together to form a one-person show.

Again, it is helpful to find an overarching theme to your stories to piece them together. You can make a cut of the door at the theater. You can tour with your show as well.

6. Tour the public-speaking circuit telling your story.

Colleges, conventions, service clubs, business networking groups—you name it! Many companies and organizations use public speakers who are candid about their own lives. I remember going to see everyone from former *Real World* cast members to feminist activists who came to speak when I was in college. A wonderful former student of mine, Caitlin Brodnick, is now a popular public speaker on breast cancer awareness and prevention.

> Having a show get canceled is like, "Oh, you have caviar between your teeth," you know what I mean? Because you had a show in the first place.
>
> **—JONATHAN AMES,**
> **writer, on the cancellation of his**
> **HBO show *Bored to Death***

I agree 100 percent with the above quote from Jonathan Ames. Any opportunities that arise from telling stories are a privilege. I always tell my students, "Act like you want to be onstage! There are hundreds of people in this city alone who would kill for the opportunity to have just five minutes of stage time."

Storytelling is an art form first and foremost. Later, you can transform it to a business, if that's what you desire. But most it should just be done for the fun of it, not for financial or career gain. To be honest, those "If it's not fun why do it?" bumper stickers used to really piss me off when I'd see a car drive by with one while I wiped off slimy tables at my thankless survival job as a waitress. I'd think to myself, "Some of us have to do un-fun things to pay

STORYTELLING ISN'T A GET-RICH-QUICK SCHEME

our bills." I now think about this quote when I'm filling out a tedious medical form or on hold with Sprint customer service. I'd love to rip up that medical form or hang up on Sprint and go, "Not fun! I don't have to do it!"

But I do believe "If it's not fun why do it?" definitely applies to storytelling. If a storyteller is no longer having fun telling stories and is more caught up in winning competitions or looking for opportunities storytelling can get them, the joy is gone and it's no longer fun to watch that person perform.

I've seen this happen to people. I even almost had it happen to me. There's an urban legend that when it comes to Moth storytelling competitions that the person who goes first is cursed. That person usually gets a low score and never wins. This is actually not true all the time—there are definite exceptions—but I would agree that it happens a lot. And wouldn't you know, at my first Moth GrandSLAM in Los Angeles, I was picked first. I was so mad, because I knew it meant I wouldn't win. I huffed and puffed my way onstage and was anything but diplomatic about it. And my performance completely lacked fun. My scores were the lowest I had ever received, and I was really bummed afterward.* The silver lining of the night was that one of my

---

* There is no video or recording of this performance online; I made sure of it!

former students won, which was joyous and rewarding to see, but after that night I really had to take a step back and think about why I do this. Yes, many opportunities have arisen for me from storytelling and it's great to win, but is that all that matters? Shouldn't I be having fun onstage even if there is no prize at the end of it?

> If it's not fun why do it?
> **—JERRY GREENFIELD,**
> **cofounder Ben & Jerry's**

That show was a wake-up call. I have not yet won the Moth's grand prize in Los Angeles (it took me years to win it in New York City), and that's fine. I've been able to tell stories on a multitude of shows and podcasts, and I can safely say that even if my stories fall flat, I still have fun. I recently had a week where I was lucky enough to perform in six different storytelling shows in seven days, and I felt like each show was a total privilege to be on. Even the show where my chin started bleeding midstory because I had gotten a mole removed that morning and decided last-minute to take off the bandage before hitting the stage. I thought the bandage would be "distracting," but nothing was more distracting than the blood dripping down my face and chin while I tried to recount a funny story about my days as a substitute teacher.

May I remind you: "Most events in life can be categorized in one of two ways: a good time or a good story."

RESOURCES

Many years ago, I randomly bought the book *I Love You More Than You Know* by Jonathan Ames because I liked the cover. It was filled with stories so personal I couldn't believe someone would be so brave to put them on paper for all eternity. Then I visited my parents in New Jersey and picked through their bookshelf when I was bored. *Monster in a Box* by Spalding Gray was the least intimidating book to try and get through that weekend, as it was the thinnest. The book was just one long personal story. I didn't even know that was a thing that could be printed as a book.

Those two books inspired me to eventually publish a book of my own stories. Other writers have greatly inspired me—Dan Savage, Charles Bukowski, David Sedaris, David Rakoff—but I often wonder, had I not read those first two books that introduced me to first-person narrative, would I have been so curious about live storytelling? Would I have found my own voice had I not been introduced to the voices of others through the written page? So get inspired. Read, read, read!*

---

* I am only recommending resources that I have actually read, watched, listened to, etc. So use this list as a guideline, but certainly seek resources outside of it.

BOOKS WITH VIVID & PERSONAL STORIES

MEMOIRS

- Paul Feig's *Kick Me: Adventures in Adolescence*
- Amy Poehler's *Yes Please*
- Rachel Dratch's *Girl Walks into a Bar ... : Comedy Calamities, Dating Disasters, and a Midlife Miracle*
- Elna Baker's *New York Regional Mormon Singles Halloween Dance*
- Dave Hill's *Tasteful Nudes: ... and Other Misguided Attempts at Personal Growth and Validation*
- *Rob Delaney: Mother. Wife. Sister. Human. Warrior. Falcon. Yardstick. Turban. Cabbage.*
- Ophira Eisenberg's *Screw Everyone: Sleeping My Way to Monogamy*
- Sara Barron's *People Are Unappealing: Even Me*
- Mike Birbiglia's *Sleepwalk with Me: and Other Painfully True Stories*
- Carlos Kotkin's *Please God Let It Be Herpes: A Heartfelt Quest for Love and Companionship*
- Chuck Klosterman's *Killing Yourself to Live: 85% of a True Story*

ESSAY COLLECTIONS

• Jonathan Ames's *I Love You More Than You Know, My
Less Than Secret Life*, and *The Double Life Is Twice as Good*
• David Sedaris's *Holidays on Ice* (includes "SantaLand
Diaries," as referenced in Chapter 2), *Dress Your Family in
Corduroy and Denim* (includes "Repeat After Me," as referenced in Chapter 11), *When You Are Engulfed in Flames*,
and *Let's Explore Diabetes with Owls**
• Chuck Klosterman's *Sex, Drugs, and Cocoa Puffs: A Low-
Culture Manifesto*
• Nora Ephron's *I Feel Bad about My Neck: And Other
Thoughts On Being a Woman* and *I Remember Nothing:
And Other Reflections*
• Anything by the late David Rakoff

STORY COLLECTIONS

• *The Moth*, edited by Catherine Burns, which includes
stories by former student Erin Barker and *Stripped
Stories* alums Jon Levin, Andy Christie, Elna Baker,
Jillian Lauren, Ophira Eisenberg, and Brian Finkelstein
• *Things I've Learned From Women Who've Dumped Me*,
edited by Ben Karlin

---

* Just read everything by David Sedaris or, better yet, listen to the
audiobooks if you really want to hear a living legend tell a story.

- *Mortified: Real Words. Real People. Real Pathetic.* Edited by David Nadelberg
- *Rejected: Tales of the Failed, Dumped and Canceled,* edited by Jon Friedman

MONOLOGUES BY SPALDING GRAY

- *Swimming to Cambodia*
- *Monster in a Box*
- *It's a Slippery Slope*
- *Gray's Anatomy*
- *Morning, Noon and Night*

BOOKS ABOUT SPALDING GRAY

- *Life Interrupted: The Unfinished Monologue**
- *The Journals of Spalding Gray,* edited by Nell Casey
- *Spalding Gray's America* by William W. Demastes**

STORYTELLING ORGANIZATIONS

I am sure there are more organizations beyond the ones I am citing, but these are some that I have had personal

---

* Gray's last monologue, with a section of eulogy pieces by those close to him.

** Includes a great history of storytelling.

experience with. I am a firm believer in creating your own opportunities if there are none in your area. So for those of you not located in these places, start your own storytelling organization!

- **The Moth** (Boston, Chicago, Denver, Dublin, Houston, London, Los Angeles, Louisville, Miami, Michigan, Milwaukee, Minneapolis/Saint Paul, New Orleans, New York City, Philadelphia, Pittsburgh, Portland, San Francisco, Seattle, Vermont) *TheMoth.org*
- **First Person Arts** (Philadelphia) *FirstPersonArts.org*
- **All For One** (New York City) *AllForOneTheater.org*
- **Barefaced Stories** (Perth, Australia) *Barefaced.com.au*
- **Porchlight** (San Francisco) *PorchlightSF.com*
- **The Story Collider** (New York City) *StoryCollider.org*
- **LA Story Works** (Los Angeles) *LAStoryWorks.org**

STORYTELLING CLASSES

The places that offer storytelling classes are ever changing. Some places offer them for a limited time; others will start offering classes after this book is printed. What I am excited to report is that classes are popping up

---

* Also runs the LA Storytelling Festival

everywhere! So if there isn't a class in your area, hopefully there will be soon. And there are teachers (like me!) who may be happy to fly out and teach a course if asked.

- Magnet Theater, New York City
- The iO West Theater, Los Angeles*
- San Francisco Comedy College**
- Upright Citizens Brigade Theatre Los Angeles***
- Upright Citizens Brigade Theatre, New York City****
- First Person Arts, Philadelphia
- All For One, New York City
- The Nerdist School, Los Angeles
- Writing Pad, Los Angeles
- The Story Studio, New York City, Los Angeles, and online
- Barefaced Stories, Perth, Australia
- Get Storied, online *GetStoried.com*
- Big Blue Door, Charlottesville, Virginia*****

---

* Taught by me.
** Taught by me—one-day workshops a few times a year.
*** Taught by me.
**** Taught by me a few times a year.
***** Taught by former student Joel Jones, as referenced in Chapter 13.

FILMS

I mention a lot of films in this book that wonderfully exemplify storytelling principles. *The Wizard of Oz, The Shawshank Redemption,* and *Ferris Bueller's Day Off* are movies to rewatch and spot the principles I describe. The three movies below are intentionally about storytelling and also worth a watch if you have time.

- *And Everything Is Going Fine,* directed by Steven Soderbergh*
- *Swimming to Cambodia,* directed by Jonathan Demme
- *Mortified Nation,* directed by Michael Mayer

STORYTELLING PODCASTS

There are many, many storytelling podcasts you can discover with just a little research. Here are a few as a launching point, but this is a genre wealthy with stories.

- *This American Life*
- *RISK!*
- *UnFictional*
- *The Moth Podcast*

---

* A fabulous documentary about Spalding Gray.

STORY RECORDINGS

YouTube has an abundance of storytelling on it. You can even learn from the bad storytelling you watch. I've made a lot of very close friends who are superb storytellers, and many of them have audio or video recordings available online. There are too many of those people to list here, and I don't want to run the risk of friends wondering, "Why did she include so-and-so and not me?"* So instead, I'm going to play it safe and give you some well-known storytellers and recordings to familiarize yourself with, and hopefully when you fall down that rabbit hole of clicking on just one more story, you'll discover some of my lesser-known but equally brilliant friends.

• *David Sedaris Live at Carnegie Hall***

• Dan Savage's "The Cat Came Back" from *This American Life*.*** Also his story about *The Suite Life of Zack & Cody* on *This American Life*'s "What I Learned from Television" episode

---

* Answer: Because I have a two-year-old and I'm sleep-deprived and sometimes I forget things.

** I cannot recommend this enough. I learn something new about this craft every time I listen to this. "Six to Eight Black Men" is so funny as told/read by Sedaris that my face hurts from laughing every single time.

*** Such a darkly funny story

- Starlee Kine's story about Phil Collins on the "Break-Up" episode of *This American Life*
- Jay Mohr's story "Summer Lovin'" on the *RISK!* podcast*
- Mike DeStefano's Moth story "Franny's Last Ride"

LIVE SPECIALS

Solo shows and storytelling-based live comedy specials are everywhere. Netflix and YouTube are great resources for these. Also, check your local theater listings for live autobiographical solo shows by some lesser-known performers too.

- Mike Birbiglia's *My Girlfriend's Boyfriend* and *What I Should Have Said Was Nothing*
- Carrie Fisher's *Wishful Drinking*
- Julia Sweeney's *Letting Go of God* and *God Said, Ha!*

---

* I have been lucky enough to be present on two different occasions to hear Jay tell this story live, and I think it's one of the funniest things I have ever heard.

ACKNOWLEDGMENTS

Special thanks go out to all my former students who inspired me to put my lessons onto the page. Thanks to my firecracker of a literary agent, Brandi Bowles of Foundry Literary + Media; to my badass TV lit Ava Greenfield at ICM; and to my latest addition Kevin Parker at Rain Management Group. A great big thank-you to Hannah Elnan, my editor at Sasquatch Books, for guiding me to this much-more-fun version of my original book idea. Thanks to Becky Donohue for suggesting that I begin teaching in the first place, many moons ago. Thank you to the Upright Citizens Brigade Training Center for hosting my classes in New York City, and for helping me create and grow my practice. Thanks to the brave outside-the-box thinkers at Universal McCann in both New York City and Los Angeles, for seeing how much storytelling could benefit the corporate world and for having me be a guest star at your company for all these years. Special thanks to Kasha Cacy in New York for being ingenious enough to bring storytelling to the company in the first place, and to Edar Lee and Karen Hunt in Los Angeles for diligently continuing the workshops in my newish home base. Thanks to my usual Los Angeles spots for teaching,

Johnny Meeks at the Upright Citizens Brigade Theatre Los Angeles, and to George McAuliffe at iO West. A big thank-you to Andrea Gibbs and Kerry O'Sullivan for creating the opportunity for me to go to Perth to teach this art form, help with the foundation of Barefaced Stories, and be inspired by Australian culture. Special thanks to Erin McGown for her assistance in a multitude of ways on this project, to Nadia Vazquez for her web design, to Mindy Tucker for her fabulous photos, and to Michael Robinson for her unbelievable talent in hair and makeup. Big thanks to Amber Eyerly for her assistance in the PR department, Emma Reh in the editing department, and to Karolyn Gehrig for generously hosting my private classes for the past few years. Thank you to Mike Still at the UCB Theatre, Los Angeles, for being so supportive of live story-telling as a part of the UCB calendar. Thank you to Joel Jones for letting me reference his deeply personal story in this book. Additional thanks to Drew Cohn, Nathaniel Cocca-Bates, Danielle Perez, Giulia Rozzi, Brian Finkelstein, and Brian Neufang for letting me use tidbits of their stories as teaching examples in this book. Thank you to the Los Angeles businesses that were generous enough to let me sit for hours working on this book: The Village Bakery and Cafe in Atwater Village and H Coffee House in Los Feliz. A big thank-you to Golden Sol Yoga for teaching me the art of stillness and meditation, which was tremendously helpful throughout the process of writing this book. There were much fewer panicky moments for this one than during the creation of my first book! Thanks to my parents and brother for encouraging me to find my own strange path at my own pace. And lastly, thank you to my husband and son for inspiring great stories daily of our adventures in this life together.

ABOUT THE AUTHOR

Margot Leitman is a storyteller, comedian, and writer originally from Matawan, New Jersey. She is the author of the comedic memoir *Gawky: Tales of an Extra Long Awkward Phase* from Seal Press/Perseus Books, which was called "hilarious" by *New Jersey Monthly* magazine, and really, who doesn't desire to make their home state proud? For television, she has written for NBC, the Hallmark Channel, and the PixL network. In print, her writing has appeared in *Playgirl* magazine and *New York Press*, and on websites such as the Frisky, CollegeHumor, and MyLifetime.com. Margot is a five-time Moth StorySLAM winner and was the Moth GrandSLAM champion in New York City in 2011. She travels all over the world performing her true stories and teaching others to tell their own. She is also an amateur baker and keeps an avid yoga practice. She lives in Los Angeles with her husband and son.

To book Margot for a storytelling workshop or speaking appearance, please visit **MargotLeitman.com**.